Tiruray Justice

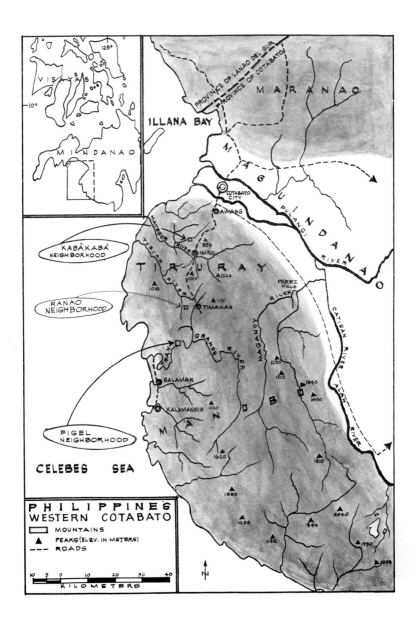

128°

VISAYAS

-10°

MINDANAO

ILLANA BAY

PROVINCE OF LANAO DEL SUR
PROVINCE OF COTABATO

MARANAO

MAGUINDANAO

COTABATO CITY

AWANG

KABÀKABÀ
NEIGHBORHOOD

TIRURAY

NURO
654

AWANG RIVER

TUBAK RIVER

1040

1226

PEREZ HILLS

PULANGI RIVER

CATIGAN RIVER

RANAO
NEIGHBORHOOD

1010

TIMANAN

1130

GRANDE RIVER

MAGANOY RIVER

TRAN

SALAMAN

KALAMANSIG

1040

MANO

B

1290

1510

1640

1690

TRAN RIVER

FIGEL
NEIGHBORHOOD

1620

1510

ALAH RIVER

CELEBES SEA

1680

PHILIPPINES
WESTERN COTABATO

MOUNTAINS
PEAKS (ELEV. IN METERS)
ROADS

1236

1122

1340

2040

1750

1095

10 5 0   10   20   30   40
KILOMETERS

N

TIRURAY JUSTICE

TRADITIONAL TIRURAY LAW AND MORALITY

STUART A. SCHLEGEL

UNIVERSITY OF CALIFORNIA PRESS

BERKELEY, LOS ANGELES, LONDON *1970*

University of California Press
Berkeley and Los Angeles, California

University of California Press, Ltd.
London, England

Copyright © 1970, by The Regents of the University of California

International Standard Book Number: 0–520–01686–6
Library of Congress Catalog Card Number: 72–107660

Printed in the United States of America

To William Scott Chalmers

CONTENTS

ACKNOWLEDGMENTS

THIS book could not have been completed without the help of many people and institutions, and I am grateful to them all.

Above all, I am indebted to the Foreign Area Fellowship Program of the American Council of Learned Societies and the Social Science Research Council for the generous grant which made possible a six-month period of research and study at the University of Michigan prior to going to the field, twenty-two months in the Philippines, and a year of writing. Some additional research expenses were covered by grants-in-aid from the Department of Anthropology of the University of Chicago.

Lloyd A. Fallers, Fred Eggan, and Bernard Cohn followed my progress from beginning to end and contributed many helpful comments. For their interest and concern as well as for their careful reading of the initial draft, I am truly thankful. A later stage of the manuscript was read by Charles Frake and Laura Nader, both of whom contributed valuable suggestions, for which I am grateful.

The number of people who helped me along the way is immense. I would like to thank particularly Professors David Steinberg and Aram Yengoyan of the University of Michigan for the many informal discussions which contributed so much to my preparation for this research. The staff of the Institute of Philippine Culture at the Ateneo de Manila was instrumental in easing the paperwork involved in entering the Philippines and again in leaving for home, and I appreciate all that they did.

The delightful Simeon Bonzon family in Cotabato City and my old friends, the George Harris family of Upi, all contributed much warmth and pleasure to off-hours during this most recent stay in the

Upi-Cotabato area. For their kindnesses and for those of the Edwards family, on whose land my family lived, I am grateful.

Carlos and Priscilla Concha put me up again and again as I passed through Lebak en route to Figel neighborhood, George Panasigan took me in for almost a month in Ranao, and Francisco Tenorio not only welcomed me as a long-time guest in his home in Kabakaba but recorded many data for me concerning his neighborhood. I thank them all.

Two Tiruray men—Mamerto Martin and Aliman Francisco—worked with me as field assistants during the entire Philippine period of my work, and without them I would have been lost. I hope they enjoyed our two-year association as much as I did and that they got out of it at least some fraction of the great good they put in.

Finally, I wish that I could thank each Tiruray by name. From 1960 to 1963, I was principal of a high school in Upi, so I have worked with and among Tiruray now for more than five years, and my affection and regard for this warm, delightful people is beyond either measure or expression.

Santa Cruz, California   S.A.S.
July 1969

KEY TO ORTHOGRAPHY

IN THE presentation of Tiruray terms, the following symbols are used to represent the six vowel phonemes and the sixteen consonant phonemes of the language.[1]

Vowels

i   voiced, high close, front, unrounded vocoid
é   voiced, mid open, front, unrounded vocoid
e   voiced, high close, mid, unrounded vocoid
a   voiced, low open, mid, unrounded vocoid
u   voiced, high close, back, rounded vocoid
o   voiced, low close, back, rounded vocoid

Consonants
Voiceless stops
t   alveolar, lightly aspirated
k   velar, lightly aspirated
ʔ   glottal

Voiced stops
b   bilabial
d   alveolar
g   velar

Voiceless fricatives
f   bilabial
s   alveolar, grooved
h   glottal

1. Tiruray phonology has been analyzed by Ursula Post of the Summer Institute of Linguistics and described in Post, "The Phonology of Tiruray," from which this key has been adapted.

Voiced nasals
m   bilabial
n   alveolar
ŋ   velar

Others
l   voiced alveolar lateral
r   voiced alveolar vibrant (trilled fluctuates freely with
       flapped)
w   voiced nonsyllabic bilabial vocoid
y   voiced nonsyllabic palatal vocoid

The high front and back vocoids are interpreted as the vowels *i*
and *u,* respectively, when they occur as syllable nuclei and potentially take stress; when they occur in the structural position of consonants, they are interpreted as the consonants *y* and *w,* respectively.

Primary stress falls on the penult or antepenult of polysyllabic
bases, except when the vowels of those syllables are shortened, in
which case stress is on the ultima. When reduplication results in
two identical closed syllables in a base, both receive primary stress.
Secondary stress may occur on words of four or more syllables,
and falls on the second syllable prior to the primary stress.

Stress in Tiruray is noncontrastive and nonphonemic, and is not
indicated in the orthography.

Tiruray Justice

Chapter 1   The Tiruray

THE TIRURAY are a hill people who live in relative though decreasing isolation in the mountains of southwestern Mindanao in the Philippines. Although the Tiruray are now under widespread and deep-reaching forces of acculturation, the traditional life of the tribe is still being lived in the far interior of the forests. In their mode of establishing and dissolving contractual relationships, and in their methods of coping with disputes and conflicts, these traditional Tiruray have developed an indigenous legal system of great elegance and of considerable comparative interest. The purpose of this book is to describe, in at least outline form, the shape of that system and, in at least illustrative manner, its substance.

Before turning in subsequent chapters to matters of morality and law, I shall, in cursory fashion, introduce the Tiruray homeland, their social organization, and their culture.

The Tiruray live in the northern part of the Cotabato Cordillera, a range of mountains which curves along the southwestern coast of Mindanao facing the Celebes Sea. Cotabato is the largest of the fifty-six provinces in the Republic of the Philippines and one of the most striking frontier areas of the nation.

Throughout Cotabato province, one can find representatives of all four of the principal subdivisions of Philippine ethnic diversity:

lowland Christians, lowland Moslems, hill peoples, and Chinese. The latter, in Cotabato as elsewhere, are widely spread throughout the peasantized regions of the country, where they dominate the wholesale and much of the retail trade.[1]

Lowland Christians have come into Cotabato province in large numbers seeking homesteads and fresh beginnings on land more fertile and less populous than their places of origin on Luzon, the Visayan islands, or northern Mindanao. Coming from regions that have been hispanized for centuries and under American influence for fifty years, the homesteaders have brought with them their Roman Catholic faith, their Westernized dress, their concern for at least a modicum of education, and their growing commitment to Filipino nationhood, centered in Manila and expressed through municipal governments and law courts throughout the land.

In Cotabato, these Christian homesteaders have settled, however, in the native territory of the Maguindanao Moslems, the feared "Moros" of old. Maguindanao is the ancient name of the area at the delta of the Pulangi—or Rio Grande—River (Saleeby 1905:13, 14; de la Costa 1961:152, 299) where this immense river system, the largest in the Philippines (cf. Irving 1952), drains into the Celebes Sea and where Cotabato City stands today. By the fifteenth century, all the lowland populations of the Cotabato Basin had been converted to Islam and had submitted to the suzerainty of the Sultan of Maguindanao, a hegemony which the Spanish were never able to destroy until the late nineteenth century when they brought steam-powered gunboats upon the scene (Saleeby 1905:16, 52).

The Maguindanao had never managed to conquer or convert the pagan hill people of the Cotabato Cordillera. There are three linguistically and geographically distinct tribes in the mountains: the Tagabili to the south, the Tiruray in the northern hills, and the Cotabato Manobo in between. These people have long traded with the coastal folk, carrying down beeswax, rattan, tobacco, and other valued products from the mountain forests and swiddens and returning with the iron tools so necessary for their upland slash-and-

---

1. On Cotabato ethnic diversity, see Hunt (1954). For the historical background of the Chinese population in Cotabato, see Wickberg (1965:22, 92).

burn agriculture, with salt, and with various other coastal and lowland goods not available in the hills. Tiruray produce neither their own pots nor their own cloth, obtaining both through trade with the Maguindanao.

Tiruray, like other non-Christian Filipino peoples, are Malay in physical appearance and speak a vernacular which, although not mutually intelligible with those of the neighboring tribal and peasant groups, is structurally very similar to them and to the other Philippine languages of the Malay-Polynesian family (Conklin 1952, 1955). Origins of the different ethnic groups in the Philippines have long been a matter of much controversy over little data. Linguistically and racially, the Philippine peoples are clearly related to each other and to the rest of the Malay populations of Southeast Asia, and there seems to be no cogent reason to doubt that the Tiruray, like the other hill peoples of the archipelago, are, at least in part, surviving representatives of the sort of culture that was widely distributed in the Philippines prior to the arrival of the strong Spanish and Islamic influences.

The mountains and valleys of the Cotabato Cordillera are neither very rugged nor very high. They are, however, covered with dense tropical evergreen forest, wherever recent plow agriculture and logging have not replaced the trees with farms or savannah. One large river, the Tran Grande, and numerous smaller ones snake their way west to the sea or east to the lowlands of the richly alluvial Cotabato Basin, collecting as they go the drainage from the many creeks and streams that lace the Cordillera (cf. Irving 1952). Rainfall in the area averages from 200 to 250 cm a year, and, although the periods from February to April tend to be somewhat warmer and drier and from June through July, more rainy than the average, still the rains are sufficiently well distributed throughout the year that the mountain streams are seldom dry. The government's climate map depicts the area as having "no very pronounced maximum rain period and no dry season" (Commonwealth of the Philippines, Commission of the Census, Manila, 1940). Travel through the mountains is slow and difficult, but not really unpleasant. Even within the forests the mountains are cooler and less humid than the adjacent coastal areas.

The country traditionally occupied by the Tiruray is not extensive, nor are the people numerous. Since the end of World War II some Tiruray have dispersed and are themselves homesteading in the lowlands or in what was once the land of the Manobo to the south. But until this century their own land was the northern part of the mountains, bounded on the west by the Celebes Sea, on the north and northeast by the end of the mountains, on the southeast by the Maganoy River, and on the south by the lower Tran Grande as it winds almost due west to the sea. The 1960 census reported 26,344 native Tiruray-speakers, the vast majority of whom remain in the mountains (Republic of the Philippines, Department of Commerce and Industry, Bureau of the Census and Statistics 1962).

By the last decades of the nineteenth century, the Spanish had established a garrison in Cotabato City, and the Jesuits had opened a mission and school for the Tiruray in the Tamantaka area at the foot of what they called the Tiruray Mountains near Awang (Saleeby 1905:15). Spanish presence was short-lived, and it was not until the time of American occupation that the Tiruray mountainous redoubt was opened to significant outside influences. The Spanish padres at Tamantaka did, however, convert a number of Awang Tiruray families. One of the first natives to be baptized, Sigayan, wrote a fascinating, if sketchy and superficial, account of the customs of his people—the first "ethnography" of the Tiruray (Tenorio 1892.)[2] Aside from passing references in Jesuit reports (Jesus, Compañia de 1877, 1880, 1883, 1887, 1889, 1895) and brief mention in several early surveys of Philippine ethnic variety (United States Bureau of the Census 1903, Beyer 1917, Savage-Landor 1904, Sawyer 1900), the only other descriptive account, prior to my own work, was a short survey of Tiruray folklore and customs by Grace Wood, based upon her fieldwork in the early 1950s (Wood 1957).

Americans first came upon the Cotabato scene early in the twentieth century in pacification campaigns against the Maguindanao. Their policy was described in 1930 by the colorful adventurer, F. D. Burdett, as "a licking from the Dough-boys, followed by a

2. For linguistic studies by the Jesuit padre at Tamantaka, see Bennasar (1892a, 1892b, 1893).

square deal by the Governor." One of the early doughboys, a Philippine Constabulary officer, Irving Edwards, took a great interest in the Tiruray and married a young woman of the tribe. He became affiliated with the Philippine Department of Education and lived on among the Tiruray until his death in the late 1950s. Captain Edwards devoted himself unceasingly over the decades to the furthering of schools and of "law and order" among the Tiruray. In 1916 he established a public school at Awang and in 1919 opened an agricultural school in Upi, near Nuro, and built a winding road from Awang up to the new school. The road now goes deeper into the mountains to a point beyond Timanan. During the 1920s many additional schools were started in areas of Tiruray occupation, and numerous lowland Christians, mostly from the Ilocano region of Luzon, began to move up into the Upi valley as homesteaders. Captain Edwards was successful in persuading many of the Tiruray in the area which runs from Awang up to the Upi plateau around Nuro to give up swidden agriculture in favor of sedentary plow farming, as practiced by their new Ilocano neighbors. This policy was aided by the Upi Agricultural School, which introduced Tiruray to the care and use of the carabao as a work animal, and by the efforts of the municipal government, headed by Captain Edwards, to register and title homesteads for both lowlanders and Tiruray. Although a large number of Tiruray retreated from the new people and new ways in the Upi valley, many stayed there and have settled into an increasingly peasantized way of life.

In 1926, at the call of the captain, the Philippine Episcopal Church established a mission with a resident missionary priest in Nuro and began a widespread string of chapels and preaching stations in nearby Tiruray communities. Episcopal work has remained strong in the area, and today six to eight priests—several of them Tiruray—hold services in more than fifty places, mostly Tiruray (cf. Schlegel 1963). Nuro, since the end of World War II, has become the center of vigorous Roman Catholic activity among the homesteader population. Like the Episcopalians, the Catholics operate medical facilities and an academic high school in Nuro, and the Roman church has recently begun a number of primary schools for Tiruray.

During the 1920s, a few Maguindanao Moslems began to take advantage of the pax Americana by moving into the mountains to settle, joining the homesteaders in what before United States control had been a strictly Tiruray area. The immigration of Maguindanao settlers became much heavier during the next decade, and with Philippine independence after the war their noble—or datu—class took control of municipal political power in the Tiruray section of the Cotabato Cordillera as well as in the Maguindanao lowlands. It has been observed, quite correctly, that when disputes occur in Cotabato, homesteader Christians turn to law, whereas the Maguindanao turn to force.[3] On the whole, the Tiruray have gotten along well with the homesteaders, but Tiruray-Maguindanao relations have long been strained. Before the coming of "law and order" under the Americans, the Tiruray were able to fight off any Moslem penetration which had any purpose other than peaceful trade. An unsought, but actual, effect of the American presence has been the ultimate Moslem take-over of Philippine political offices in the area and the attendant legitimization of Maguindanao power. Many Tiruray who had settled permanently onto a piece of land have since been forced off or have abandoned their farms to retreat deeper into the mountains from their Maguindanao neighbors, preferring to give up their homeland to surrendering their traditional isolation and way of life. Others have become homesteaders themselves down on the Basin plain.

Today, therefore, Tiruray are not everywhere alike. In common with so many ethnic minority groups around the world, they are undergoing rapid change in their social and physical environment and in their way of life. Those living in the northernmost areas of the mountains, from Awang to approximately Timanan, have now known more than half a century of intense contact with lowland peasants—both Christian and, more recently but significantly, Moslem—and with American military, educational, and missionary enterprises. Some have fled up-country, but most from that area have experienced severe acculturation. They have become plow farmers; they have been drawn much more deeply into the cash, credit, and

3. "When conflict arises, the Christian (lowlander) resorts to courts of law and the Moro to guerrilla attacks," (Hunt 1957:19).

market economy typical of Filipino peasant life; they have learned to speak the local form of the (basically Tagalog) national language. These modernized or peasantized Tiruray have turned from their older religious ways and leaders to Christianity, following clergy who are either American missionaries, Filipinos from Luzon, or profoundly Westernized Tiruray. They attempt, at present, no leading role in local or national politics, but they constitute an important part of the constituency of those Maguindanao or homesteader leaders who do.

In marked contrast, however, are those Tiruray who live so deep in the mountains or so far up the Tran Grande River that they have not been significantly affected by the various acculturating forces. These people—probably numbering about 10,000—still live the traditional tribal life.

The Tiruray recognize their own ethnolinguistic distinctiveness and refer to themselves collectively as the Tiruray people (*ʔetew teduray*). They loosely subdivide themselves, according to their general geographic location, into mountain people (*ʔetew rotor*), coastal people (*ʔetew dogot*), Tran people (*ʔetew teran*), and Awang people (*ʔetew ʔawaŋ*). The latter have in recent years come to be known also as people of Upi (*ʔetew ʔufiʔ*) as, with the building of the road and the establishment of Upi-Nuro as a market and municipal center, the Awang population has spread out to include the Upi valley.

These subdivisions do not delineate discrete groups. A man of Timanan may be considered an Upi person by the people along the Tran and a mountain person by those in Awang. Nor, with the exception of Awang, are they in any sense distinct subcultures. From centuries of contact and military alliance with the Maguindanao, the Awang area has long tended to have a higher prestige among Tiruray than the others, its people have displayed more internal social ranking, and its culture has incorporated some distinctive customs of Moslem origin. In general, however, the Awang are much the same as the other Tiruray. A few words are considered coastal, but the language too is essentially identical throughout the Tiruray area.

The greater part of my study of traditional Tiruray life was done in Figel, a neighborhood of people from along the Tran Grande. The "neighborhood" (ʔiŋed) is the largest social unit with discrete boundaries. A neighborhood consists of a number of families which regularly assist each other in their swidden agricultural activities and rituals, and thus determines an agricultural cooperation group. Any Tiruray can easily name the households and settlements which comprise his own neighborhood. While it is not an attribute of the neighborhood that its members should be linked by kinship ties, either consanguineal or affinal, it is usually the case that almost all are.

The history of the neighborhood of Figel is quite typical of how such communities come into being. About 1800 a man known as Moʔembot (father of ʔEmbot)[4] came to the narrow place (figel) in the Tran Grande where Figel settlement stands today. He brought his family with him, and many of his descendents have remained in Figel and have brought in spouses from elsewhere. Today there are three heads of households in Figel neighborhood who are fourth generation male descendents of Moʔembot. Nine current heads of households are fifth generation male descendents, and two household heads are married to fifth generation female descendents. Five heads of households are sixth generation male descendents; two are married to sixth generation females. These families all consider Figel to be their ancestral place and speak of themselves as ʔetew figel. Other descendents, both male and female, have married or migrated to other locations, of course; there is no semblance of any descent group structure among the Tiruray. Residence after marriage is predominantly patrilocal, that is, in the place of the husband's parents, although there are instances of matrilocal residence, especially when the man's kindred has not been able to complete the brideprice given for his wife. Neolocal residence also occurs, when there is felt to be an important economic advantage to being elsewhere than with either the man's or woman's parents.

Those who trace descent from Moʔembot may be considered

---

4. In Tiruray teknonymy, the 'Father of . . .' is called *Mo* . . . ; the 'Mother of . . .' is *ʔIdeŋ* . . . . Teknonyms are extremely common, and throughout I use them as Tiruray do in naming all those who are not more commonly known by some other name or title, for example, Balaʔud (Molamfiton), the major legal authority of Figel.

to form a core line in Figel. The leader of the Figel neighbors is a renowned legal authority (*kefeduwan*) known as Bala?ud, whose father was a mountain person that married into the Figel core. Bala?ud's father was a highly respected kefeduwan throughout the Tran area, and Bala?ud himself had gained a reputation for legal wit and acumen when he was still very young. In 1951 Mo? inugal— a first cousin of Bala?ud through their fathers, and a person of Upi —came to Figel and settled among his cousin's followers. With regard to Mo?inugal, the Figel core line people were mostly in-laws. He had left Upi because of the troubles with outlaws and bandits that had occurred in the wake of World War II. A few years later, a first cousin of Mo?inugal and Bala?ud followed for the same reason and settled in the Figel neighborhood. In 1958, still another family joined Mo?inugal, being stepparents of his wife. These moves were intended to be permanent, and the people involved henceforth considered themselves to be people of Figel.

All who live in a single neighborhood are said to be *setifon,* an expression which means literally 'of one house' and which seems to reflect an earlier period when neighbors all lived in a single large house. Now, although Bala?ud still occupies an enormous house, large enough to sleep all in Figel neighborhood, with the more peaceful times which began under American control individual families have started living in their own houses. The big house is still considered, in a sense, however, to be the real home of all the neighbors, and all consider themselves to be setifon. Those persons who are setifon with the people of Figel, but who are themselves people of another place who are in Figel because of marriage to a Figel person, are called *meŋgeselet,* 'grafted-in.' A person or family that is setifon in Figel but is not related to the others—either by blood or by marriage—is said to be *meŋgerafu?,* 'a fallen tree,' in the place.

In 1965 Mosew, one of the important religious leaders (*beliyan*) of Figel today, came to live in Figel, like the others to escape trou-blesome outlaws in Timanan, his previous home. Mosew is the husband of a woman whose daughter by a previous marriage was a 'grafted-in' wife in Figel neighborhood. With him came three other households: two married sons and a married stepson.

A few months later, still another household came to Figel to flee from troubles in the peasant areas. In this case, the family head's wife was the sister of a 'grafted in' wife of a fifth generation man of the core line.

Thus, no families in the Figel neighborhood are meŋgerafuʔ, although there is no reason why a family that is in no way related should not settle among the Figel people. Should such a family wish to do so, and were they prepared to share in the cooperative agricultural activities on the swiddens of Figel neighbors, they would be welcomed as new people of Figel.

The people living in any neighborhood do not reside in a central village, but in settlements (deyonon), small dispersed hamlets of from one to twenty houses—three to six being most common. Although every farmer must associate himself with others in a neighborhood, he need not live in company with others in a settlement. Of the seven settlements that comprised Figel neighborhood at the time of my census in 1966, two had only one household each; one had three households; one, four; two had six; and one had eight. In general, any household is free to establish its residence in any settlement it wishes, and no standards exist to structure a settlement on any kinship principle, but usually some relationship, either affinal or consanguineal, links the families that settle in the same hamlet. Households that live alone in a settlement are thought to be a bit strange, and the neighbors of such a family often speculate that they are stingy and unwilling to share with settlement mates or are difficult to get along with. Much sharing goes on among the households of a settlement. Fish caught in the river are always shared, as are snack foods such as roasted corn or fruits. Chickens, eggs, and rice are never shared, except in ritual meals or with visitors, as they symbolize the discreteness of every subsistence family. In contrast, the flesh of a deer or wild pig caught in hunting is always shared throughout the entire neighborhood, with each individual family receiving almost exactly an equal share; these catches symbolize the cooperative unity of the neighborhood—a unity that is also expressed in the rice exchanges which are characteristic of the Tiruray ritual neighborhood feasts.

Settlements are named after prominent geographical features

nearby; Figel, for instance, means a narrow place in the river. A neighborhood is named either after its principal settlement (like Figel) or after the foremost legal authority of the neighborhood (the people of Figel are referred to as Balaʔud's people). Tiruray, if asked where they are from, will reply with the name of their neighborhood either by place or by leader, and not by naming their settlement. The latter do not have the stability of location or household composition of a neighborhood and tend to shift around as the people look for better spots or abandon a location that is associated with an illness or a death. Neighborhoods, and not settlements, are the important and relatively stable territorial units.

The residential unit and fundamental social building block is the household. In most cases, the household is composed of a single nuclear family which eats from a common pot—the word for family being *kureŋ* ('pot'). In some cases—there is one such in Figel neighborhood—an unmarried and dependent elder is included in the family. A polygynous household will contain a man who is a member of as many pots as he has wives. Only two of the twenty-nine Figel neighborhood households were polygynous at the time of my census; in each case, the man had "inherited" his second wife through the operation of a system of spouse replacement at death. There is no limit to the number of wives a man may have—and thus the number of families to which he may belong—but he must care for all of them satisfactorily and equally well.

Rarely, a single house will contain two households; there were three such cases in Figel neighborhood. This can occur, for example, when a newly arrived household has been unable yet to erect its own house, or when a couple is newly married and has still not put up its own dwelling. Such arrangements are always considered to be temporary and irregular.

When children from a pot marry, they are in a new family, and they eat from a new pot. Relations between households may be by kinship or by brideprice contract or by agricultural cooperation, but the households are very much independent, self-determining units. Should a father and his married son cooperate in working on their respective swiddens, they do so merely as neighbors.

The household, whether monogynous or polygynous, has the

fundamental and corporate economic responsibility of feeding and provisioning itself. All property and any money—as well as all crops—are owned by the household for its common use. In the case where there is more than one wife, the senior (first) wife is the chief spokesman for all the other women with regard to the economic tasks, responsibilities, and rights within their household.

Traditional Tiruray obtain certain items from coastal markets, but on the whole they subsist on the proceeds from swidden agriculture, from hunting and fishing, and from extensive gathering of wild foods. The agricultural cycle of swidden activities is timed by careful reference to the location in the night sky of several constellations and follows a yearly sequence (Schlegel, in print). Late in December or early in January, the farmers ritually mark their swidden sites for the coming cycle and begin the heavy labor of cutting away the dense jungle undergrowth and felling the massive trees. The men of a neighborhood work on each household's site in turn, and by March or April all sites are ready to burn. The swiddens are first planted—by men and women together—in corn and several varieties of rice. Several other crops are planted at the same time around the edges of the site. By May or June the first corn crops are harvested by the women and stored; by August or September the rice is ready to be harvested. The rice stalks remaining are cleaned away, and tobacco or a second crop of corn is planted, as well as more tubers, fruit, vegetables, spices, and such nonedibles as cotton. These crops will be harvested as they are mature and needed, but the field will not be further prepared or planted until it has lain fallow for many years, so that the vital jungle vegetation may be reestablished.

The men, whose swidden work is largely finished when the fields are well prepared and planted to corn and rice, devote much of their time through the rest of the year to hunting, fishing, and gathering wild foods from the jungle. Many kinds of traps, snares, and weapons are utilized, and a very broad subsistence base of wild and domesticated plant and animal food is regularly exploited. Tiruray are expert with the blowgun, the bow and arrow, and the hunting spear, to which since the war they have added the homemade shotgun. Hunting dogs are kept and trained to see and corner game in the forests.

Certain items—especially salt, iron tools, ceremonial exchange items, and cloth—are obtained in markets along the coast, usually in exchange for rattan and other forest products. Traditional Tiruray are familiar with cash and use it in the market but very little elsewhere. Cats are kept around the houses as mousers and, like the dogs, are never eaten. Chickens and pigs are also maintained, the former primarily for eggs and ritual meals, the latter primarily for the piglets which are sold or exchanged at market.

Aside from his membership in a neighborhood, every Tiruray is the center point of a personal kindred which, reckoned bilaterally from that person (Ego), includes all the descendents of his four pairs of great-grandparents and thus reaches laterally to include all second cousins. All such relatives are considered to be *segedet,* or 'close together,' with Ego and constitute his exogamic range within which a marriage would be considered incestuous (*sumbaŋ*). Third cousins and all other descendents of great-great-grandparents, are considered *serayurayuʔ*, 'further apart from each other'; marriage is permitted, but a special item of brideprice must be given by both of the contracting families in order to render the union free of incest. Still more distant consanguineals—and all to whom Ego can trace no blood relationship—are termed *serayuʔ*, 'far from each other,' and may marry freely.

The group of segedet consanguineals which comprise Ego's kindred have important responsibilities toward him or her and are mobilized on behalf of Ego in disputes whether they are settled legally or by feuding, at the establishment of a family through marriage and the giving of brideprice, or at the dissolution of a marriage by death or divorce. If a Tiruray finds himself involved in a feud, he expects all in his kindred to come to his assistance, and, similarly, he has placed them all in danger of attack. Should the dispute be settled legally rather than by feuding, the person's kindred shares in paying the fine if Ego is judged responsible or in the distribution of the fine received if Ego "has the right." At the time of marriage, a man's kindred is called upon to join in con-

tributing brideprice items, and the legal leaders within his kindred
assist in establishing the marriage. The bride's kindred shares in the
establishment and in the distribution of the brideprice. At the time
of a person's death, his kindred is summoned to share in the seven
days of funeral rites and in their cost.

Being Ego-centered, the personal kindred is, of course, different
for every sibling group and is not itself a corporate group. Most
importantly, his kindred is that roster of humans amidst which a
person feels most secure and safe. Among Tiruray, great danger
and risk are assumed in all other personal encounters. Only among
close blood relatives is it believed that one is fully free of the threat
of violence. An individual's kindred is concerned. His acts of brav-
ery, generosity, or some other recognized virtue bring great pride
to them; any publicly known misbehavior brings them a sense of
shame. His kindred are those with whom, in several senses, Ego is
close.

Terminologically, the Tiruray kinship system is bilateral and
quite uncomplicated. Tiruray kinship terms give emphasis to the
central importance of the nuclear family—the pot—by singling out
the consanguineals of the pot into which Ego was born (his family
of orientation) and that which he creates by marriage (his family
of procreation) with special referential terms, as follows: *ʔeboh,*
'father'; *ʔideŋ,* 'mother'; *ʔofoʔ,* 'older sibling'; *tuwarey,* 'younger
sibling'; and *ʔeŋaʔ,* 'child.' Otherwise, all close consanguineals in
Ego's grandparental generation and above, or his grandchildren's
generation and below, are referred to as *bébéʔ,* 'grandparent' or
'grandchild.' All other close males in the parental generation are
referred to as *momoʔ,* 'uncle,' and all other close females in that first
ascending generation as *ʔinaʔ,* 'aunt.' All close relatives of ascending
generations are referred to collectively as kindred 'elders,' *lukes.*
Close blood kinsmen in Ego's own generation—other than his
siblings—are called *dumon,* 'cousin,' and no distinction is made
between cross and parallel cousins. All close first generation descendents except Ego's children are referred to as *ʔonok,* 'nephew'
or 'niece.'

In short, the members of one's nuclear families of orientation
and procreation are set off from all others in one's kindred, and

the latter are distinguished by generation but not according to descent.[5] Any blood relative, whether close or not, may be called Ego's *lusud,* and any close blood relative may be called his *dumon* (the word here being used at a different level of contrast than when it means 'cousin').

By use of the modifier *tintu,* 'genuine' or 'real,' Ego's actual parent's parents or his children's children may be identified as *tintu bébéʔ,* his parent's siblings as either *tintu momoʔ* or *tintu ʔinaʔ,* and, in like manner, one's 'real' nephews or nieces—children of the 'real' aunts and uncles—may be specified as *tintu ʔonok.*

With regard to affines, Ego's 'spouse'—either husband or wife—is referred to as *bawag,* and Ego refers to the 'spouse's parents' as *terima,* a term extended to all close blood elders of the spouse. Ego's child's or grandchild's spouse is referred to as *ʔawas,* 'child-in-law,' and the parents of the *ʔawas* as *belaʔi,* 'co-parent-in-law,' this term also being extended to include all close consanguineal elders. To distinguish the actual parents of the *bawag* or the *ʔawas,* the *tintu* may be used. A man and his wife are said to be *sebawag,* 'married to each other,' and the two sponsoring kindreds which entered into the brideprice relationship are referred to as *sebelaʔi,* 'co-in-laws of each other.'

In a polygynous household the husband and each of his wives are sebawag, but the first wife is distinguished as the *tafay bawag,* 'senior wife,' and each other wife is referred to as *duwoy,* 'co-wife.'

5. The following four distinctive features establish the consanguineal contrasts: generation [G], degree of collaterality [C], sex [M or F], and relative age [A^+ = elder, A^- = younger]. Using these symbols, the consanguineal terminology of reference may be summarized as follows:

	C¹	C²	C³	C⁴
$G^{\pm 2}$	*bébéʔ* →			
G^{+1}	*ʔeboh* (M) *ʔideŋ* (F)	*momoʔ* (M) *ʔinaʔ* (F) →		
G^0	EGO	*ʔofoʔ* (A^+) *tuwarey* (A^-)	*dumon* →	
G^{-1}	*ʔeŋaʔ*	*ʔonok* →		

A polygynous marriage is contracted and established with the same procedure as a first marriage and creates a new pot—the parents of a duwoy are Ego's *terima,* those of a child's duwoy are *bela?i.*

In Ego's own generation the affinal terms of reference, other than those of spouse or co-spouse, make a distinction according to whether the relationship is between males. A male Ego speaks of his wife's brothers or male cousins and of his sister's or female cousin's husband as his *?efél,* 'sibling-in-law'; he refers to his wife's sisters and female cousins and to his brother's or cousin's wives as *?ibo?.* A woman refers to any of her husband's siblings or any of her siblings' spouses as *?ibo?.* The term *idos,* 'co-sibling-in-law,' is used in reference to one who is joined to Ego by two affinal links, being married into the same family that Ego is related to by marriage, for example, spouses of Ego's spouse's siblings or cousins.[6]

In direct address, parents are called by their referential term, and all other elders, whether related or not and without regard to kindred limits, are called by the term of reference appropriate to their generation and sex: 'grandparent,' 'uncle,' or 'aunt.' There is strict avoidance of the use of a generational elder's personal name. Ego addresses his siblings and all other close consanguineal peers or

6. The following distinctive features establish the affinal contrasts: (1) point of affinity [$P^=$ = ego; $P^\vee$ = descendent], (2) generation [$G^=$ = same generation as the point of affinity, G^+ = ascendant generation from point of affinity], (3) degree of affinity [D^1 = one affinal link, D^2 = two affinal links], (4) complexity [C^- = simple, joined to Ego by affinal links only, C^+ = complex, joined to Ego either by (a) one affinal link plus one or two collateral degrees, in that order, or (b) one or two collateral degrees plus one affinal link in that order, and (5) genders involved [M^+ = both males, M^- = not both males]. Using these symbols, the affinal terminology of reference may be summarized as follows:

	P	G	D	C	M
terima		+			
bawag				−	
?ibo?	=	=	1	+	−
?efél					+
?idos			2		
bela?i	↓	+			
?awas		=			

juniors by their names. One's spouse is also called by personal
name. All other affinally related peers are addressed by use of the
referential terms, and all others of Ego's generation by their teknonym—'Father of X' or 'Mother of X'—or by the general expressions ʔadih, 'friend' (used only between males), or ʔawé?, 'friend'
(used only between females). In reference, anyone may be called
by his or her teknonym.

In terms of behavior, the closest relationship of all is that of
man and wife; this is the heart of the pot. One's parents are, of
course, in their own family; one's children will marry out and establish their own households. Only the married couple—so long as
they and the marriage live—are permanently in the same pot.
Moreover, the division of agricultural labor between men's work
and women's work makes it virtually mandatory that every farmer
have an active wife and that each adult and active woman be wedded to a working husband. It is the fundamental importance of
husband and wife to each other which yields the great concern in
Tiruray society for the establishment and repair of viable marriages,
and which helps to make selamfaʔ, 'elopement with a married person,' a serious moral offense. To Tiruray one's spouse has sole right
to sexual access; there are no mistresses and no prostitution.

There are several possible motives for a man to take a second
wife. In most cases, he is accepting the widow of a close relative.
Other circumstances however are possible. A man may wish the
additional prestige and sexual satisfaction that a new young wife
would bring. Or he may be trying for children, if childless with his
first wife. The first wife has the right of giving or withholding
consent to his taking any particular duwoy. There are advantages
in the arrangement for her: she can share the harder work with
another, she can have the help of a younger woman, and she can
have additional companionship in her day-to-day tasks. Not infrequently, it is the wife who suggests to her husband that he might
wish to marry again.

When there are co-wives, the first wife—the tafay bawag—is the
leader of the others. She assigns them their work around the house
and sees to their doing their share in their husband's fields. The entire household—the man and all his wives—are the joint owners

and workers of all fields; all produce is owned in common by the
household, and the foods are distributed to the various pots by the
first wife. The husband has no set place to sleep, but goes from wife
to wife in rotation, according to the arrangement made by the first
wife. He must follow this scheme. How long he stays with one and
how long with another is up to the tafay bawag; any arrangement
is all right that does not hurt her feelings. Similarly, the second
oldest wife is next to be satisfied with the arrangement. The husband may sleep most of the time with a young, vigorous wife—but
only if the more senior wives are happy about it.

Parents are completely responsible for their children and may
not ask help in their care from the grandparents, who are felt to be
busy with their own concerns. The mother will suckle the child until
it is two or even three years old or until another baby comes. She
generally keeps her suckling child right with her, carrying it on her
hip or in her arms when moving about and hanging it from a tree
trunk in a sarong when working in the fields. The child is given the
breast whenever it cries, but on the whole the parents do not seem
to direct much attention to their children. Once they can walk, they
play around the settlement quite on their own with little supervi-
sion. As soon as they are old enough to give token help, they are
put to work with their parents. From about the age of six, children
join their parents in farming activities or in playing near the swiddens. Boys are sent to gather firewood, to take care of animals, to
fish, to hunt wild birds with the blowgun, to guard the swidden
from monkeys, and so forth. Girls are set to pounding rice, to weav-
ing rattan baskets, to fetching water from the river or spring, to
washing clothes. In all of this there is little formal instruction; the
children learn by imitation, by trying, and by helping. By the time
they are adolescents, they do the same work as their parents do and
have absorbed the skills they need to function as Tiruray adults.

Parents administer discipline to their children with scoldings,
slaps, pinches, and whipping with a stick, according to the severity
of the offense—or, more precisely, according to the irritation of
the parent. The spanking and harsh scoldings invariably come when
the child has directly and personally irritated his parent or some
other elder, just as fights with their siblings or peers come from

doing some directly irritating action to them. Children soon learn
the cardinal rule of Tiruray human relations—do not make anyone
angry at you. There are few or no formal standards of behavior
imposed on a child, with this or that being good or bad for him, and
there are no rules about when to sleep, about when or what to eat,
or about where to play. The main thing is not to antagonize anyone
or there will be trouble! Beyond trying to guide their children into
good social relations and away from physically dangerous situations, parents are, on the whole, permissive and indulgent.

Being members of different pots, children do not look to their
uncles or aunts for advice with their problems; they are merely
close elders. There is no special visiting to their houses, as there is
none to the house of grandparents. There is no particular feeling
of being any closer to them emotionally than to any other elders.
As a man or woman grows older, of course, all in his or her kindred
do assume an important legal role.

Siblings are close companions when they are young, they fish
and play together or in groups of other children. But age difference
is of great importance. They must be respectful all the time to older
siblings—just as to an uncle, except that they may use the personal
name of their older sibling, but never of an uncle. Adolescents com-
plain that they cannot have any fun around siblings because they
always are reporting to the parents, and I have spoken to no grown
Tiruray who says that he would want a sibling as a close friend or
chum. Once a sibling is married, he is close as a relative but usually
is treated with the same deference and independence as any other
individual in a different family. Brothers are, of course, extremely
close kinsmen and share interests, but otherwise after they have
married they are emotionally neither particularly close nor especially distant.

Because of the general feeling that one must take great care in
dealing with nonkindred individuals, relations with Ego's in-laws
are attended to with prudent caution. A boy's parents, in choosing
a woman to marry their son, apply many criteria. They are concerned that she be the same age or younger, that she be industrious,
that she seem healthy and courteous. Beauty is not too important;
she should not be disfigured, but there is a general feeling that a

woman who is too pretty will not want to work hard under the hot
sun. Above all else, the girl's parents and other close relatives
should be desirable as in-laws. This last consideration is by far
the most important. The marriage will bring two kindreds into affinal relationship, and it is of serious consequence if they should
not get along well.

Tiruray say that it is better to have a trouble with your own
brother or sister than with your sibling-in-law. The feelings of your
own blood kin will not explode so quickly, and anger, if it is present,
will not last so long. People will thus go out of their way to seem to
be good in-laws; they will occasionally do things not required by
custom of an affine, but only of a blood kinsman, such as helping
with brideprice payment or the giving of a fine.

A girl who has reached marriageable age but is not yet married
is called a *kenogon;* a boy not yet married but of age is called a
kenogo lagey. In both cases, the person is known to have come of
marriageable age by the development of secondary sexual characteristics. When this has occurred, the kenogon and kenogo lagey are
expected to act henceforth as adults. Their teeth are filed and
blackened, they begin to chew the betel leaf mixed with areca nut,
tobacco, and lime, and they dress in adult clothing.

Traditional Tiruray men wear closely fitted trousers and tunics.
Women wear sarongs and skintight blouses. Not having cut their
hair since they were a year old, men and women alike have long
hair. The women pull their hair straight back, tying it with a knot
in back of their heads. Men wind their hair round and round their
heads and secure it in place with bandannas. The sarong serves as
a sleeping wrap for both men and women. On special occasions,
such as a wedding or an agricultural community feast, a woman
will use a more expensive cloth for her sarong and wear a beaded
necklace; men carry krises, the wavy-bladed swords which, like
the necklaces, are of lowland Moslem manufacture and originally
obtained from coastal markets.

Once a girl has become an adolescent, she is very closely watched
by her elders, who want to keep her from any sexual activity before
marriage. Young, unmarried boys are regarded as irresponsible and
difficult to control. Thus, as soon as possible the elders of young

adults seek to arrange marriages for them. Tiruray lore maintains that in the "old days," weddings were accomplished for young children—the child wife being raised by her young husband's parents until the two were old enough to maintain their separate household. While this may have been so before, postpuberty marriage is today everywhere the practice.

One's kindred is most visibly mobilized at the time of marriages, disputes, and deaths. Tiruray marriage is a relationship entered into by two kindreds, on behalf of a man and a woman. It is symbolized by the man's kindred's giving an aggregate of formal property items —*tamuk*—as a brideprice to the woman's kindred. The marriage is arranged by formal meetings between the two involved kindreds, without the knowledge of the couple to be wedded. Similar formal meetings between involved kindreds occur when two individuals or groups of individuals become involved in a dispute. In this situation also tamuk passes hands, not as brideprice but as fine. Such formal encounters between two or more kindreds are known as *tiyawan,* and the actual speaking during the proceedings is done almost entirely by a class of tiyawan specialists called kefeduwan. Kefeduwan are the society's recognized legal and moral authorities. The body of this book is devoted to a description and analysis of tiyawan and of the work of the kefeduwan in arranging contracts and settling disputes.

It is characteristic of tiyawan that on one level they are concerned with tamuk, a class of property items which, in addition to their practical everyday usefulness, have great symbolic value. Considered as tamuk are krises (*sunday*), gold and glass bead necklaces (*kemagi*), fancy working bolos (*tabas*), fighting spears (*dilek*), vases (*biay*), small China plates (*bilew*), brass betel quid boxes (*tegu?an*), sets of small Tiruray gongs (*?aguy*), large Maguindanao-style gongs (*dakel ?aguy*) fancy sarongs (*?emut*), animals (*?ayam*)—usually carabao or zebu working animals—and money (*filak*). With the exception of the animals, all of these tamuk items originate outside of Tiruray society; they originally come in through trade with the coastal or lowland Moslems and then change ownership frequently as they are utilized as brideprice payments or fines.

It is not possible here to present the rich and complex imagery of traditional Tiruray cosmological and mythical beliefs. It should be said, however, that not all tiyawan occur between humans. Tiruray understand the universe as being populated with a vast number of types of *ʔetew*, 'people,'—some of which (*keʔilawan*, 'humans') can be seen and others of which (*meginalew,* 'spirits') cannot be seen without a special charisma. The spirits are organized in tribes and, in general, go about their business—coinhabiting the universe with the humans. Some spirits are naturally cruel and malignant in their relations with humans, as, for example, are the *busaw,* a tribe of spirits that live mostly in caves who eat the *remoger* ('soul') of any human they can trap. Others are by nature kind to the humans, as, for example, the chief of all the spirits, Tulus, or his messengers, the *telaki*. Most tribes of spirits, however, are—like humans—composed of individuals who are friendly enough if they are not angered in some way, but who can be dangerous indeed to a human that offends them.

Tiruray understand their relations with the spirits as being quite the same as their relations with other humans. The cruel, dangerous ones should be avoided whenever possible and guarded against by the use of charms and amulets. With other spirits, one should simply strive to have good interpersonal relations. The problem is that the spirits cannot be seen by the ordinary fellow. Thus, altercations do arise between spirits and humans, the practical effect of which is that the human becomes ill. In such circumstances, he has need of a *beliyan,* 'religious leader.'

The beliyan's particular ability is a gift from the spirit world of being able to see spirits and thus being able to talk to them. He is therefore able to seek out the spirit with whom his ill human follower has fallen into dispute and bring the issue to its spirit beliyan. The matter is then settled between them in tiyawan. The beliyan is, thus, a very special kefeduwan—one who settles tiyawan that occur between spirits and humans. The various tribes also have their kefeduwan who handle tiyawan among their own kind. They have beliyan to settle tiyawan between their spirit followers and other kinds of spirits or humans. Thus, in terms of interpersonal relations, Tiruray extend both their moral prescriptions and their legal institutions to a superhuman, cosmic level.

A final comment is in order before I close this brief and general introduction to the Tiruray people. Between the two extremes which I have mentioned—the traditional tribesmen and the acculturated peasantry—one does not find a marked cultural fault line, but rather a wide area of greater or lesser contact and involvement with non-Tiruray institutions and patterns of interaction. During the more than half-decade that I have been traveling about through a great variety of Tiruray settlements and through areas where Tiruray families live amidst other sorts of settlers, I have been forcibly struck by the fact that the transformation of traditional, tribal Tiruray society into one of the peasant segments of the larger Filipino society is an ongoing process along a continuum of increasing structural realignment, stretching from the still isolated people I have termed traditional, through various gradations of contact with outside influences and changing circumstances, to the Upi Valley and northward where the Tiruray are living a thoroughly different life than did their ancestors. Roads are rapidly being completed into the most isolated areas of Tiruray occupation, and the government estimates that the main road through Timanan will link up with Salaman and Kalamansig on the coast within five years. Schools and chapels are being erected along the roads and from them deep into the interior. Christian and Moslem homesteaders are penetrating ever farther into the mountains. Logging companies are continually exercising their government franchises to cut away more and more of the forests. Such trends as these are intricately interrelated with each other and with other political, economic, and social factors which have emerged in the past half-century since American hegemony over both mountains and flatlands first broke the isolation of the Tiruray and opened their cordilleran redoubt to outside interests and influences. Here, it is not possible to go into details of that history, but I can say that it seems very doubtful that in another twenty years it will be possible to locate a single Tiruray community where isolation and ecological conditions remain to permit the traditional Tiruray way of life (Schlegel 1968). A once viable mountain tribe—now caught up in the waves and currents of what we speak of as history and judge to be progress—is rapidly becoming fragmented into an array of individuated peasant families.

Gone with the forest are the rich rewards of hunting and gathering, as well as the swidden mode of agriculture. The legal system which, with juristic elegance, knit together these forest farmers, and a religious system which projected their legal and moral concepts to a superhuman plane of social relations, are both vanishing entirely, and with them, the influential legal and religious leaders so crucial to the fabric of the old Tiruray culture. The people are becoming, in short, ever less Tiruray and ever more Filipino.

Chapter 2　　　　　　　Tiruray Morality

I spent most of the morning speaking with an old man about
the customs (*ʔadat*) surrounding a wedding ceremony. He
asked at one point whether I had ever seen a Maguindanao
wedding and explained that they have a very different set of
customs which comes out of their written law (*kitab*). "The
Maguindanao have their Koran," he said, "but we cannot read
or write; our kitab is the ʔadat."[1]

TO TIRURAY, in one fundamental sense of the word, the ʔadat of
a people is their customs, the things they customarily do, the activities that mark them as a distinctive cultural entity. The Maguindanao
have their ʔadat; the Americans have theirs; the Tiruray, theirs.
Early in my fieldwork among the Tiruray, I learned that such questions as "Why do you do that?" or "Why is it like that?" or "Why is
it done in that fashion?" were all one-way, dead-end streets leading
to the inevitable reply, "It is the ʔadat." They do what they do, in
the way they do it, because it is the Tiruray custom to do it, and in

---

1. Throughout this book, indented extracts not otherwise identified come
more or less directly from my field notes. Most of what was recorded in the
Tiruray vernacular I have translated into English, and I have made a few
editorial improvements in the original prose.

that way. Why do Tiruray press hands one way when departing, whereas American shake hands a different way when they leave? Because each has his own ʔadat.

ʔAdat, however, has another fundamental meaning: respect. In this sense, it can be used not only as a noun but as a verb, meaning to pay respect to someone or something. The two senses, custom and respect, are by no means discrete for Tiruray; they are aspects of a single idea. The customs aim at respect. Respect is what customs are for. It is, in fact, what customs are—ʔadat. One can speak of an individual's ʔadat (or a family's) with the same combined meaning, both of someone's characteristic behavior and of the quality of his respect for the feelings of other people. Frequently I have heard it said that some marriage is a difficult one because one of the couple has a bad ʔadat, even though the person comes from a family known for its good ʔadat. When the marriage was arranged, it is implied, there was nothing in the respectful, considerate ways of the errant spouse's parents and kinsmen to warn the prospective in-laws of the bad manners, hot temper, snobbery, or whatever—the disrespect of others' feelings—that was to be revealed in the newlywed.

There is still a third significant element in the notion of ʔadat. It is normative; it includes the idea of "ought." A tribe's, family's, or individual's ʔadat may be contrasted to its tufuʔ, another term which has the English sense of custom or habit. If a man wears a mustache, that is his tufuʔ. One who goes regularly at a certain time each morning to check his pig has developed a tufuʔ to do that. Some families have the tufuʔ to give or to ask working animals as part of a brideprice; other families have the tufuʔ not to; still others are indifferent to the question—they have no tufuʔ on that matter either way. The critical difference between tufuʔ and ʔadat is that the latter has a normative content, whereas the former has none. A man's habits in the care of his pig or the wearing of a mustache are his own concern; a family may decide for itself whether it wishes to give or to ask carabaos. ʔAdat is not involved in the custom, as it is not one which bears upon respect for other people; and no moral obligation is implied.

Of course, ʔadat is certainly involved in how people deal with someone's particular tufu?. The decision to wear a mustache is tufu?; not to make a derogatory comment about someone else's mustache is ?adat.

Bala?ud told a story about the importance of respecting the tufu?. There was a family, whose tufu? was to ask carabaos as part of a brideprice. They were arranging a marriage between their daughter and the boy of a family whose tufu? was not to give animals. What happened was that they asked for one animal, and the boy's side gave one, but the girl's side immediately gave one kris, which they called a *teleb sogo,* 'to cover over the footprints,' which is to say, to hide the carabao's having been given. That way neither side was forced to break its tufu?. The girl's side considered the carabao as part of the brideprice; the boy's side did not, but looked upon it as a gift. It was remembered, but not formally counted in their reckoning of the settlement. Several years later, the girl ran away with another man, and the brideprice had to be returned. A carabao was returned, of course, but it was called a *ruranan tamuk,* 'to carry the brideprice items.' Thus the woman's side considered that they returned the carabao, but the other side looked upon that animal as having merely borne their goods back to them. That is the way, Bala?ud said, we show ?adat; one must always observe the ?adat.

For Tiruray, then, the ?adat is not only (like tufu?) what they, as Tiruray, do and how they do it (their customs with regard to weddings, newcomers, labor exchange, and the like). It is also (unlike tufu?) what they ought to do and how they ought to do it. The ?adat sets standards of conduct; it places obligations—all of which are seen in terms of interpersonal respect.

As I have mentioned, an aspect of the Tiruray world view underlies this overwhelming concern for respectful behavior. Like that of all peoples, Tiruray culture sets forth a world in which everyone understands himself to live, a world whose nature is taken for granted.[2] Thus, to Tiruray there are certain "facts" about the nature

2. The term "world" is here understood in the phenomenological sense. For extended discussions of the world as one's phenomenal, taken-for-granted sphere of reality, see Schutz (1962) and Berger and Luckmann (1966).

of this world, about mankind, and about social life which they understand as being simply and self-evidently true. One such fact is that men are, by nature, potentially violent. Men are capable of exploding under provocation into a fury of bloodshed and vengeance. Why this should be so is not at issue here; to Tiruray it *is* so, and men *are* that way.

Furthermore, one is especially likely to burst into violence when outraged by a nonrelative; one is, by nature, less apt to feel hatred toward a kinsman in the first place and, if he should do so, is far more able to contain his inherent propensity to lash out violently. Thus it is a fact of life to Tiruray that the world of interfamilial social relations is one of danger, potential bloodshed, and continual risk and that amidst one's kinsmen there is mutual assistance and a context of relative safety. A father may attempt to give moral advice or a mild scolding to his son, but the world "being as it is," only a madman would scold a nonkinsman and incur the inevitable retaliatory consequences.

However much an anthropologist or a sociologist may demonstrate that other men in other lands do not understand human nature in this way, to the Tiruray themselves those propositions about the nature of man and society are simply true. They are objective realities of the Tiruray common-sense world. To behave in violation of their normative implications would not merely show bad taste, it would flout the fundamental canons of common sense so thoroughly as to suggest utter insanity.[3]

For Tiruray, as for the participants in any culturally given and shared world view, their taken-for-granted world is their paramount reality—the foundation of their everyday awareness and the matrix from which common sense is established as the natural attitude toward day-to-day affairs, that is, as the primary model for pragmatic action in the world.[4] It is the peculiar function of common sense that it embraces the apparent givenness of the seemingly real in both its cognitive and normative aspects, and thereby sets forth a

3. The fundamental role of common sense has been profoundly analyzed by Schutz; see especially (1962:3–47).
4. The term "paramount reality" is from Schutz; see (1962:207 ff.). My discussion has been importantly influenced by Geertz; see especially (1958, 1964a, 1964b, 1966).

model for prudent behavior in daily life—a model which is rooted
both in that which "clearly is" and in that which "clearly ought to
be." The violent propensities of human nature, the security that pre-
vails among kinsmen, and the perils of social intercourse outside
one's family are, to Tiruray common sense, not matters for specu-
lation. They are cognitive facts. And, similarly, the conviction that
only an appropriately related elder ought to engage in scolding
someone—and then only with utmost care—is no mere rubric of
etiquette but a normative fact, a moral truth proceeding from what
Tiruray understand to be the very nature of man.

Thus, respect for others is the Tiruray's most basic moral obligation—the essence of his tribal custom and the guiding intention of
behavior felt to be most distinctively Tiruray. Thus, too, a world in
which the sensitivities of all are respected by all is the society's most
compelling moral goal. Only such a social situation can be assessed
as good, as right, as being "the way it should be"—as being, in the
fundamentally important Tiruray concept which sums up all such
ideas, *fiyo*.

A thing is fiyo when it is just the way it ought to be. A woman
who has physical beauty according to Tiruray canons (light skin,
shiny long black hair, thick ankles, a narrow waist) is, with regard
to her appearance, fiyo. More generally, a woman, however plain,
who works hard, who is kind, who is modest, who thus meets the
more important and serious canons involved in judging female quality, is also fiyo. The weather is fiyo when it is clear so that one can
do his work. A decision is fiyo when it is made with sensitivity and
sense. One who has been sick is fiyo again upon recovery. A fiyo
homemade shotgun is one that shoots regularly and accurately. A
meal is fiyo if it tastes good and is filling. Ubiquitous in Tiruray discourse, the term can range over a vast number of connotations for
which English has separate words, such as proper, delicious, attrac-
tive, adequate, convincing, right, and good. Its opposite, *tété?*—as
commonly used and as widely applied as fiyo—denotes anything that
is bad, wicked, ugly, defective, or, in sum, anything that is in an
important way not as it should be, that is fundamentally, profoundly amiss, that is not fiyo.

The "good world" is one, then, in which as much as possible is fiyo. Tiruray realize, of course, that there are limits and bounds to the human capacity to bring about the good and that not every aspect of existence can be always fiyo. Good weather is bound to alternate with bad. In a forest existence, there inevitably are times when the stomach is too empty and the muscles are too tired. They fully expect that death will inflict grief and that childbirth will bring pain. Life's hardships are beyond human control. But many misfortunes are not; they are believed to have a personal cause. People (whether humans or spirits) are apt to react with violence against anyone who injures them in body or in feelings. Thus in one vastly significant area of life, human behavior can and must be channeled. People must be obliged to respect each other's normally placid, but inherently dangerous, feelings. It is a basic premise of Tiruray common sense that only in a social order of mutual forbearance, a moral order laying upon both men and spirits the obligation of interpersonal respect, can one hope for even the most minimally fiyo world.

Much of the variety of day-to-day interpersonal contact can be structured by established tribal custom so that, in a straightforward manner, one can be respectful of his fellow's feelings by adherence to the customs. Much, but not all. Respect of each individual's feelings is the overriding goal of the ?adat, not merely scrupulous observance of tribal custom, however important the latter may seem as a means of achieving the moral goal. Thus ?adat (as respect) daily requires everyone to make decisions about right behavior in situations where the ?adat (as specific Tiruray custom) is silent. In these uncharted situations, the individual must determine for himself what course of action is morally right, what is ?adat for him at that moment and in that set of circumstances.

Respecting the feelings of others is characteristically spoken of in terms of not giving anyone a *tété? fedew,* literally, a 'bad gallbladder.' The notion of a person's *fedew* is utterly central to Tiruray moral and legal thought and must be considered with care.

The Tiruray word "fedew," like the English word "heart," on one level names an organ of the body, but, also like heart, fedew is widely extended to embrace a cluster of figurative, metaphorical meanings. The fedew in this extended sense is one's state of mind or rational feelings, one's condition of desiring or intending. Some examples may help to clarify the concept of fedew.

"What is your fedew?" asks of a person his specific desire, decision, or intention about a particular matter, as, "What is your fedew; will you go on Wednesday or Friday?" or "It is my fedew to sleep in Tagisa before proceeding."

"How does your fedew feel?" inquires into someone's mental reaction to an event and evokes such replies as, "My fedew is quite all right (fiyo)," meaning, "I am glad," "I am satisfied," "I don't mind," or "my fedew is very bad," which may indicate that the speaker is lonely or very sick and worried about his family or that he is hurt and angry because of some insult. This sense of the word appears in statements of necessary conditions for making one's fedew good again or in the gentle introduction of a kinsman to the offering of advice: "Don't have a bad fedew if I have something to tell you."

Feelings which are referred to the fedew are ones which involve active thinking—conscious mental processes. It is a mind at ease, free from disturbance, which is fiyo. In contrast, one which is distracted from its practical, day-to-day concerns and obsessed with thoughts of worry, fear, anger, hatred, and revenge is tété?, not as it should be, bad.

Two general kinds of bad fedew are distinguished, according to whether the cause was fate or the action of a person. The first, ?embuku? fedew, might be glossed as a 'painful' fedew. One is lonesome, sad, in grief, worried, or bothered with haunting envy. One feels ashamed, in the presence of someone else, of his poor house, or his embarrassing error. He feels vaguely suspicious that something is amiss, without knowing who or what is the cause. In such cases (each having its own descriptive, as memala, 'embarrassed'; ?embuku?, 'lonely,' 'grieving'; melidu?, 'worried'), the fedew is said to be generally ?embuku?, 'painful.' In such instances, although the person has a bad fedew, he does not feel anger or hatred or a drive toward vengeance. His painful fedew is caused by his fate in a difficult and uncertain world; it is bad, but it is not 'hurt'—the second kind of bad fedew—through the actions of some other person.

When a fedew is 'hurt' (*demawet* fedew), it is because the person feels that he has been abused in some way. However successful he may be in containing and controlling his rage, even in outwardly concealing it, that a person so injured will feel a deep moral outrage and hatred toward the one who wronged him and that he will inevitably wish revenge is never questioned.

> We spoke for a while about shame. He told me that it is very different to be 'ashamed' (*memala*—really more like the English "embarrassed") and to be 'put to shame' (*fenmala*). "You can be ashamed without feeling hurt and angry, although it is very painful. But anyone who is put to shame will be very hurt and terribly angry. If a big shot came to our town, and perhaps was a relative—a distant cousin, say, who was a big shot now in the city—so he came to eat at my house, of course I would be ashamed because my house is very small, poor, very humble. My fedew would be bad. But I would do the best I could to receive him. We would butcher a chicken, and be sure and obtain some rice to eat. Then, if he were to refuse my food—perhaps even comment that he feared getting sick— I would also be very hurt, so my fedew would be bad in a much worse way. I would be put to shame and very hot with anger. Of course, especially if it is my relative, I would try to hold it, but I know I would want to hit him, or do something even worse."

An ordinary person cannot help feeling embarrassed at the rustic hospitality he can offer to a prestigious, renowned, or affluent visitor, but he can expect that his guest will not insult him or put him to public embarrassment. The latter would be a clear violation of moral principle and a radically different matter. His otherwise 'painful' fedew would then be 'hurt.' He might or might not show an immediate overt reaction, but his hurt fedew would certainly be angry, and it would cry out for revenge; it would harbor henceforth a deep grudge; it would be a hating fedew. Any act is wrong which either intentionally or imprudently leads to such a bad fedew.

A bad fedew is—simply—not fiyo; it is not "as it should be." The painful fedew and the hurt fedew differ essentially in their origins and therefore in their potential danger to social harmony and well-being. The one is caused by somebody and thus brings the bad fedew into a hating relationship with another person, a situation fraught, as Tiruray see it, with danger and violence. Painful feelings are part of the unavoidable ups and downs of life. There is much that one can do through religious belief and ritual to live with them and to render them meaningful, but little that one can do to avoid them. In contrast, a bad fedew caused by human foolishness can and ought to be avoided. It is this "ought" which is conceived to be the rationale for, the meaning and end of, the customs (ʔadat). It defines respect—one ought never cause a bad fedew—and thus permits substance to be given to that most fundamental principle of Tiruray moral thought.

My traveling companion (a graduate of the agricultural high school, more given, perhaps to systematic thought than most) and I chatted at length along the way about keʔaliʔ, 'exercising care not to cause anyone a bad fedew.' As he saw it, there are three main things to respect: a person's belongings (ʔentiŋayen), his standing (tindeg), and his feelings as such (fedew). Disrespect of any of these, he felt, is what incites a bad fedew.

A person's ʔentiŋayen, his 'belongings' or 'possessions,' is all that is his, all of which he is géféʔ. To be géféʔ of something is to have exclusive rights over its present use. In peasantized areas, the actual owner, holding title to a tract of land, is the géféʔ of the land; but, if he has a tenant to whom he has assigned his land to work, his tenant is the géféʔ of the plowed field which he is working. Traditional Tiruray have no concept of permanent land ownership, but the man who cuts a particular swidden is its géféʔ and the "owner" of all that is grown upon it. When it returns to fallow, he continues to be its géféʔ in that, once sufficient secondary forest has been reestablished for the plot to be farmed again, no one may cut that area without asking him to release his rights. A man is the géféʔ of his own house, of his wife, of his work animals, of whatever property is his at any given time, of a wedding that he is celebrating for his daughter, of a legal proceeding that concerns his hurt fedew, in short, of any object, person, or event in which he has not only an economic and emotional interest, but a personal, legitimate oversight. Such things (his clothing, his family, his rituals, his property, his fields) are his for so long as his rights over them continue; they are collectively his ʔentiŋayen, and he is the géfé? of each and of all. And, my companion urged, one cannot respect the person without respecting those rights.

> Stealing (menakaw) is very bad and will surely cause a bad fedew. Getting property is hard; and what's yours is yours. It should not be taken. You take someone's property without his permission and without giving him anything—he will surely be very hot. How can people live together who do that? Rice and corn will not just grow unless they are planted. Things are owned. The géfé? is the géfé?. If you really need something or need help, just ask. Tiruray are kind; they will share. But if you take without asking, you don't respect the person. You lower his standing. He will be terribly angry.

Not respecting one's belongings thus touches another of the suggested danger areas, one's tindeg, 'standing.' The following situations all involve the notion of standing:

> There was much discussion about a religious leader from a community just over the mountains to the northeast. It seems that he called for all of his followers to gather together, and a large number did not come. They say he has a very bad fedew to those who did not come, since they did not respect his standing. Even though he is not doing anything, he is very hating. He will keep it in mind, and if they continue to act that way he will not help them when they need him.

> We had gone several kilometers along extremely mucky trails, when we came to a house, and stopped to take a drink of water. The owner asked us to come up, and I was about to do so—without thinking about the mud all over my shoes—when (my companion on the hike) stopped me gently and pointed to my feet. I removed my shoes. Later, I asked him about it, and he explained that among Tiruray to enter someone's house with muddy feet is against the customs; it is as though his house is the home of a pig rather than a person, as though

you think of him as not caring for his home; it would lower his standing.

He said the rape not only lowered his daughter's standing and put her to shame, but also his own and his whole family's standing; if the man wanted his daughter, he should have told his old folks and they could have come and arranged for a marriage in the right way.

A man's standing is, in a broad sense, his social position. It includes his relative age and authority, his relative dignity and honor, his social esteem. Everyone has his standing. Families or individuals have "higher" or "lower" standing, in the sense of their general reputations; a son who does foolish things is said to lower the standing of his family, by acting in a way more base than his relatives and forefathers have been known to act. But, in another sense, a person's standing is his (or her) "good name"—his personal, individual honor and standing among his fellows. And everyone has a right to having his standing treated with respect. However humble one's family, each person has his own good name and his right to it. He can lower his own standing—can sully his own good name—by his own actions, but he will be deeply offended if anyone else should do that to him.

The idea of standing is clearly manifested in the distinction between the Tiruray concepts of despising and of correcting or advising.

Because of the harvest, Benito (a brother of one of the wives in Figel neighborhood) and Teŋaŋa (their first cousin) were in Figel for a few days. Benito kept complaining that Teŋaŋa was lacking in dignity. He was saying that whenever there was a gathering Teŋaŋa did not sit formally but was always darting around. He gave as his opinion that when a fellow is ugly, he should at least have dignity. When these words reached Teŋaŋa, he became furious at his cousin. He went up to him and demanded, "Why do you talk about me, despising me? I will give you a good beating for your lies about me." Benito replied, "Come on and see if you can—besides it is all true— you are ugly and you are a fool." So they began to fight.

When he learned what was going on, their uncle (a considerably older man) ran over and separated them. He told them to sit down where they were, and he asked them what happened. Once they were a bit cooler, he called them aside and told them privately that both were foolish. He told Teŋaŋa that he too felt that he did not show much dignity in his blatant lack of formality; he then told Benito that he was hardly showing dignity himself in publicly despising his cousin. He advised them both that if they wanted to fight each other they should go ahead *inside* his house, among their own kin—who could see how foolish they were without having to suffer public shame—but that outside the house they had better act more sensibly, or they would end up offending some nonrelative and then would be in real trouble.

I asked the uncle, when he later described to me how he had corrected his nephews, whether they would not feel that he was despising them. He replied, "An elder close relative may give a person advice, warnings, scoldings—he can be quite frank —he has the right to do that; he has the standing. But, otherwise, to say such things to a person would be to despise him and would surely cause him a bad fedew. For example, if you were to tell me that you did not like my clothes (he was wearing the traditional Tiruray dress), it would be very bad. A person may wear what he likes to wear. You would be despising me, and I would have a very bad fedew. If you said that thing in front of others and despised me publicly, it would be far worse. My fedew would not only be hurt, but shamed."

I asked whether a person would be hurt if it was his father who criticized his manner of dress. "No, not if he told him in a nice way. That would be correcting, not despising. Even if the person disagreed with his father, he would not feel that he was hating him, but only trying to give him good advice." I then wondered what would happen if a close friend tried to offer some good advice. He looked surprised at the question. "No one would ever do that. Only relatives who are older give you advice. We never try to advise nonrelatives; we have no standing to do that. It would most certainly be considered despising." Could a nephew ever advise his uncle, for example, not to gamble? Continued curious surprise at such naïve questions: "No, no. He could never do that. The uncle would feel that his nephew did not respect his standing and would be very hurt. It is against our custom."

Several terms used in advising or scolding display the great concern for respect and the fear about the consequences of disrespect. One who is insensitive to the feelings of others is said to be not *semegafaʔ*, and elders tell children frequently that if they are not semegafaʔ they will be hated, they will find themselves in danger, they will cause great trouble for everyone. A person who does as he pleases without *any* thought for the feelings of others is called *lemigisligis,* and it is said that a true lemigisligis seldom lives to grow old. He ignores his acts of disrespect, so his acts are foolhardy; they should make him ashamed and worried, but they actually leave him unconcerned. They do not lead him to learn proper behavior, to make sensible, decent estimates of his moral obligations in the situations of daily life. Such estimates are difficult enough for the earnest person; one who ignores signs and clues that might help is either utterly foolish or mad.

An individual's estimate of a situation is the *karaŋ* of his fedew. He can have a karaŋ of whether it will rain or whether it is a good day to hunt pigs. One's estimate is, of course, crucial to his effort to behave morally. Many judgments must be made concerning a situation—what is required, what is reasonable, what will hurt, and so forth. It is the fedew which, in reaching its estimate of a situation, takes a position regarding moral obligation and the demands of respect.

My traveling companion's assessment of the general areas of moral tenderness—one's property, his self-esteem, and his social position—is no formal analysis; his categories are certainly not exclusive (to steal one's wife is also to hurt his feelings and to lower his standing), nor, probably, are they exhaustive. But if he is not a systematic philosopher, he is a morally earnest person faced with the daily problem of specifying in particular instances what is involved in respect. His categories do indicate, more than does the notion of fedew alone, how one proceeds to behave respectfully in order not to cause a bad fedew. One applies a set of ideas—ideas which to Tiruray seem sheer common sense, simply features of the way things are—of what constitutes a good fedew and of what is apt to turn it bad. One employs his general knowledge of the sorts of sensitivity to which any fedew is given and looks for specific clues to understand any particular sensitivities of the particular fedew with which he is confronted.

Communication of such clues—both sending and receiving the signals—is critically important, and a vast array of concepts in Tiruray thought are employed for this. Of the myriad, a few examples from two classes may be taken as typical. Both are classes of noun forms derived from adjectives which specify something— an object, a person, a situation—in which a specific fedew is deeply involved emotionally. Each, by setting forth some piece of public information about that fedew, serves to identify its claims upon or sensitivities regarding respect.

The first set of terms signals that someone is probably holding in strong and explosive desires; that he should be "handled with care" because his fedew is already in some internal turmoil and less than usually able to contain any subsequent pressure. Moreover, they identify the focus of the engaged fedew and warn that for the person in question it too must be treated with prudent care. Something which is causing a person profound envy, for example, is said by that person to be his 'envy object,' the ke²iŋaran of his fedew. Similarly, there are terms for that which is filling a fedew with thoughts of hatred (the *kerarekon* fedew) or which has brought someone close to the end of his patience, has rendered him "fed up" (the *kesemunon* fedew), or is the object of his serious suspicions or jealousy (the *kedalewon* fedew). These concepts provide plain public warnings about a given fedew in a given set of circumstances.

Another class of fedew-signals serves to publish an individual's claims to reasonable and specific respect from his fellows for particular concerns of his own. A plan of action that a person is known to have, some intention to do something, is said to be the *bantak* of his fedew. The intellect (*²ituŋen*) considers the plan, thinks through the details. It is, however, the fedew which feels commitment to it, and others ought to give reasonable respect to a person's plans and not complicate or obstruct them needlessly. A bantak is, therefore, publicly known information about a fedew's engagement. If you know that a man's fedew has a certain intention, you know something substantive about respecting that man; not causing him a bad fedew is given content in terms of respect for his plan of action. Conversely, of course, failure to respect his plans is specified and identified as a failure to respect his fedew.

Similarly, a ke²ika²an of someone's fedew is its known personal aversion, something that the individual really dislikes. Not all persons have the same aversion, nor do all have the same quantity of personal dislikes. One fellow's personal aversions may include a whole roster of relatively minor "pet peeves"; another's may be some single, intensely felt hatred. Whatever and however many the known ke²ika²an of an individual, those who deal with him socially are extremely careful about them, lest they set off a bad fedew.

The same is true about a known ketayan, that which a fedew especially likes or desires. In general, Tiruray feel morally obliged to grant people respect for their purely individual tastes and idosyncrasies, where they are within reasonable limits. Of course, an aversion that was utterly disruptive of normal social expectations, such as a dislike for meeting one's reciprocal labor obligations, or an equivalent personal wish, such as a desire for another man's wife, would hardly be considered by one's companions to create moral obligation. But it is also true that no one would seriously and publicly present such an outlandish suggestion as the aversion or the desire of his fedew. Both in asserting their own fedew and in attending to others', Tiruray are common participants in a general cultural consensus concerning the reasonable and sensible limits of personal demands.

The precise boundaries of reason and good sense in any given concrete situation are, however, an inevitable source of difficulty. Despite acute efforts to be morally sensitive, situations often do arise in which there can be honest and deeply felt differences of opinion about whether a particular personal plan of action has been given its due respect, whether someone's desire is beyond the limits of propriety, or the extent to which an individual's peculiar antipathy should morally obligate his neighbors to suffer sustained inconvenience.

Some guidance is provided by folk stories, such as this humorous episode in the escapades of Inoterigo, a marvelous female of "long ago":

> When Inoterigo wanted to catch some nice fish for her supper, she would go to the mouth of the river and, plugging her anus with an egg, would drink up all the water. When the river bed was dry, she could easily fill her basket with fish. Then she would vomit back the water and go home. One day, when she was fishing in this manner and had drunk up all the water from the river, a young man named Tibugel happened to pass by. He asked Inoterigo for some of her fish—because she had gotten them all—but she would not give him any, saying that it was her fedew's dislike (keʔikaʔan) to share any of her catch. So Tibugel went home. At his house, he had a pet wild rooster, which he dispatched to the river. The rooster found Inoterigo bent over, picking up fish from the river bed, and pecked the egg in her anus. The egg broke and the water all rushed out of Inoterigo. The rooster ran home to Tibugel. Inoterigo repented her foolishness and from then on would always share her fish.

Tibugel had rejected Inoterigo's personal aversion as unreasonable; she had recognized the justice of his effective, if whimsical, rebuke. The story and others like it can make the point that there are limits beyond which moral obligation is not established; but it cannot spell out for specific cases precisely what those limits are.

The 'dislike,' the 'plan,' and the 'desire' are examples of a large class of concepts which publish the presumably reasonable demands of a particular fedew in a particular situation. A fedew may also have that for which it is profoundly craving, for which it is longing. It may have its overriding concern, its absolute first priority. All such ideas give, in an overt and accessible manner, meaning and content to the general moral imperative to respect one's fellows, to avoid causing anyone a bad fedew. Concepts of this sort are necessary: tribal custom can organize vast amounts, but not all, of interpersonal behavior. And they are effective: in most cases, most of the time, claims to respect so published are felt to be well within bounds and to constitute binding moral obligations. But it is also true that in some cases, some of the time, they necessarily raise the question "at the boundary" of what is reasonable respect and what are unreasonable demands.

The Tiruray sense of moral obligation to respect each other's fedew underlies and finds expression in a normative terminology, words which might be glossed as 'right,' 'good,' 'rights,' 'fault,' 'wrong,' 'bad,' 'transgressor,' 'wrongdoer,' all of which have within their meanings a characteristic sense of *ought*—required, observed, or violated. The *ʔarus* way to do something, for example, is the best way to do it, in the sense of the most expedient, straightforward way; the *fatut* way to do it is the morally proper way, the way that is good (fiyo), that is in keeping with custom (ʔadat), the way that will not hurt anyone's fedew. A course of action may well be recommended as both ʔarus (the most practical) and fatut (the decent) approach, but the two evaluations are not the same. If a theft were planned and carried out with logic, finesse, and success, the thief might well be credited with having done his wrong in an ʔarus way. But it would not have been fatut; stealing is wrong, however elegantly done, and the victim will have a thoroughly outraged bad fedew. The former is devoid of normative content; the latter specifically applies it.

A person whose actions have caused a bad fedew is said to be *dufaŋ*, the fundamental pejorative in moral evaluation. In its various linguistic forms, the term may mean the one who makes the trouble, the wrong act itself, the doing of it, or the one against whom it is done. But in each instance the word specifies a situation in which someone has violated his moral obligation to respect another, he has caused a hurt fedew, he has done wrong. By definition and by the whole logic of Tiruray morality, dufaŋ is serious and dangerous. Acculturated English-speaking Tiruray translate it as 'foolish,' but the gloss is too mild unless understood in the sense of being utterly reckless. To act 'foolishly' is to enrage a fedew. It is, thus, certainly to upset normal social relations, and it is very possible to incur violent, bloody turmoil for oneself and for society.

Whenever one must in the course of normal activities do something which *could* imply disrespect, like walking in front of someone, passing between two people, or interrupting a conversation, custom and respect (ʔadat) call for the expression *tabiyaʔ*, which, rather like "excuse me," signals that no disrespect is intended.

He warned me about hiking along the river—one must be careful not to offend. "You may pass where a woman is bathing. If she sees you coming and knows that there is no other trail, she will take cover and not be hurt. But, it may be that she is facing the other way and cannot see your coming; you should call out, 'Tabiyaʔ, you will be seen!' Then she can cover herself. If you happen to see a naked woman—for example, if you happen upon her unexpectedly when crossing a river— you must be quick to say, 'You were seen; tabiyaʔ!' If you do not say that, she will think that you were intentionally peeping. Once you say that, even though she will be embarrassed that her body was seen, she will not be angry at you because she will know that it was an accident and that you did not dufaŋ her."

To dufaŋ is to act either with intention to do wrong or with excessive imprudence. If a group of men are working together slashing a swidden site, and the bolo blade of one breaks, flies, and cuts the flesh of a companion, there is no bad fedew. Although by custom the one who caused blood to flow will give his injured associate a token gift, he was not 'foolish'; there was no intention to cause harm. If a woman was forced into having extramarital sexual intercourse, she did not dufaŋ her husband, although her abuser certainly did. Should a man pick up someone else's property by mistake and return it, there is no 'foolishness' because no intention to steal.

The issue here is whether the act is intentional or not; it is not whether the person doing it expects to be caught:

Moʔilag and Mobayaw (two legal leaders) were chatting in Moʔilag's house one morning, where they were awaiting Motineŋka, who was expected to arrive sometime that day to ask to marry ʔIdeŋ Surut, the divorced daughter of Mobayaw. Their conversation turned to how ugly they felt Motineŋka to be, since his teeth were not kept properly blackened, but were merely yellow from betel chewing. Laughingly, they compared his teeth and general appearance to that of the man-eating giant, the *busaw*. Unfortunately, at that moment, Motineŋka happened by the house, and overheard what the two men were saying. He was extremely angry, and entering the house with his spear high as though ready to thrust, he confronted the two men and growled that he may have yellow teeth, but has not yet eaten any human being. He accused them of despising him and asked them to judge themselves. They immediately accepted their fault and placed sixty plates and two krises before Motineŋka, to restore his good fedew. With that, he cooled off and lowered his spear; soon afterwards he returned to his own place, and he sought a wife elsewhere.

Even where there is no intention to hurt, a reasonable exercise of prudence is required by ?adat, and carelessness which runs one afoul of someone's feelings is also culpable.

On arrival at Figel (after having been away for over a week), I learned that Mosew had a very bad fedew toward a youth from Tuwol. The young man had been here overnight and had been showing around his newly acquired homemade shotgun. To demonstrate the gun, he fired once into the bushes to the east of the settlement. It was dusk, and already quite dark, and he did not see Mosew walking nearby. Mosew said he was badly frightened by the nearness of the report and was almost hit by the flying pellets. He had been really upset, and, although the boy from Tuwol had earnestly insisted that he did not realize anyone was there, Mosew says that he cannot forget such foolishness.

(Several days later) ?Udoy, a kefeduwan from Tuwol, came and said that the foolishness had not been intentional but that he agreed that Mosew had the right to ask whatever he wished. Mosew said that he had been genuinely outraged by the youth's foolishness, but that he would ask only one spear.

Whenever an offense occurs and a fedew is made bad, the matter of *sala?* (fault or responsibility) and the matter of *benal* (understandable demands for retaliation, for acceptable compensation) are immediately raised. A person is *mensalaʔ*, he 'has the fault' or 'bears the responsibility' when a fedew is made bad by his 'foolish' behavior. If the one who has been hurt is a close relative, he may be expected under ordinary circumstances to hold his feelings in check until his anger toward his kinsman subsides or until an elder can correct the errant one. But, if the one hurt is not a close blood relative and his fedew was made angry, he cannot be expected to do nothing. He is hurt; his fedew hates and craves revenge, and that craving for revenge and retaliation is, to Tiruray, "human nature" and understandable. Given the hurt he has been forced to endure, it is his inevitable and natural inclination to seek redress; this is his benal. That he can be expected to strike out in vengeance against the person who committed the foolishness against him is simply and, to Tiruray common sense, obviously the consequence of 'foolish' (dufaŋ) behavior. However dislocating it is to the general social order, and however dangerous it may be for all his relatives, the individual 'foolish' enough to hurt a fedew cannot expect that suffering will not follow. He is the mensalaʔ; his victim has his benal.

I asked whether the *toʔow béʔén* (a particularly poisonous jungle snake) was considered 'cruel' (*mediyabu*), and was told a fascinating bit of "Tiruray history." The toʔow béʔén was the very first of all the snakes and was born to a Tiruray father and mother, twin to a baby boy. The boy and his snake brother always played together, and they slept on the same mat in the house. One day the boy fell dead, but the snake cured him by getting grasses and rubbing his body. The father, however, was worried and told the snake, "You had better separate from your twin; you are a snake, and the houses are for humans. The proper place for snakes is in the forest." So the boy and the snake made an agreement, promising never to harm each other as they were of the same blood. Henceforth, they would live each in his own place, and neither would go to the house of the other. A human might always go through the forest, and the toʔow béʔén will not kill him, unless he steps upon his nest; similarly, the human will not kill the snake, unless the toʔow béʔén should break the agreement and come to the house

of the human. Of course, if either trespasses their agreement—
if the human steps on the snake's nest in the forest, or if the
snake is found in someone's home—then the trespasser clearly has the fault (sala?), and the other will as clearly have the
benal to kill him. Thus, to this day, on the whole, people and
this variety of venomous snake leave each other alone. When
the snake is 'foolish' (dufaŋ) enough to come where he should
not be, of course, the people try to kill him. Similarly, when
a human is bitten by that snake in the forest, you know that
it is not because the snake was cruel—but because he had
the benal. The to?ow bé?én would not kill anyone who did
not break the agreement. It is not cruel to attack someone who
has offended you. The busaw are the cruel ones—because they
will eat you, even though you did nothing to offend them.
They attack you without benal.

One evening, one of the older men of Ranao spent some time
with me out under the stars, explaining and telling stories about
the constellations which he saw in the night sky. It was a beautiful,
warm night, and the talk drifted from one subject to another, finally
settling on difficulties that arise among neighbors and how they
should be handled so that they would not lead to serious trouble.

"My cousin and I were once living very near each other," he
told me, "and quite far from the spring where we were getting
our water. So our wives and daughters had to carry water a
great distance every day. My cousin's wife fell into the habit of
just getting water at our house, rather than carrying it all the
way from the spring. She did not do it every time, of course,
but still much too often. Pretty soon my wife had a bad fedew
to her cousin-in-law, and although she held her anger in her
fedew, she complained bitterly to me that my cousin's wife
was not respecting what was ours. I planned to speak to my
cousin and urge him to provide his own house with water, so
that our wives would not fight; this is what happens when
wives are not related—they easily quarrel. But when I went to
see my cousin, I did not have the courage to bring out my advice, so we only talked about hunting. I went to see him another time, but still could not bring this out, for fear that he

might be resentful of my words. So I went to see our uncle,
who lived fairly nearby, and I told him my problem. He
agreed that my wife might not be able to hold it much longer,
and promised to speak to my cousin. Things did not change,
though, so we built a different house farther away from my
cousin's house and there was no further trouble."

It sometimes happens that a person is very ready to call for
help with his field, but when asked to reciprocate always seems
to have something else to do. People will soon have a bad
fedew to that person. They will just hold it and not do or say
anything directly to him, although they will certainly talk about
what he does when he is not around. At first, everyone may
help him all the more—to emphasize what is right; then they
will just stop helping him. They will hold on to their anger,
because he is their *dumon,* 'relative,' 'neighbor'; but when he
calls them for help they will all say that they have other things
to do.

'Holding'—literally, 'able to hold steady'—(*getiŋkel*) is one
possible response of a bad fedew toward the one at fault. As in the
two instances above, to hold is the characteristic response to dufaŋ
behavior among close relatives. To a somewhat less predictable extent, it may be expected among nonkinsmen neighbors who are
close day-to-day associates. In general, a cool restraint of those
violent, vengeful urges considered so natural to hurt fedew is thought
to be as clearly worthy of praise as it is difficult of achievement.
Anger is conceived as engulfing the fedew in a rising crest of hatred.
It can be contained to a point. Then it will break forth in benal, in
desire for vengeance. There is an obligation to hold anger at petty
irritations, but Tiruray believe that beyond a certain point it is only
a morally heroic fedew which might be capable of bearing the re-
sentment and hatred. Everyone should hold himself as much as possible. People should not just get hot right away whenever they are
displeased, especially with close relatives. But there are limits; some
things are just too much, and anger is bound to come out. Here, as
with such ideas as the aversion of the fedew, the central point is
quite clear—people deserve reasonable respect for their aversions;

they are also expected to bear a reasonable amount of annoyance. But the matter of how much is too much, of where the boundaries of reason and sense lie, is inevitably problematic. That people *can* hold only so much is an empirical observation without normative content; that they *should* hold on to their rage to a certain extent, and that no one *should* push anyone else past that point, is an entirely normative matter. Judging what constitutes that reasonable extent is a profoundly sensitive operation.

The violence which is so feared is, indeed, another possible re-action to being morally abused. A bad fedew, pushed beyond its capacity to hold, will have the understandable benal to see vindica-tion of its honor, and it may very well go looking for blood revenge. Such killing because of moral outrage, *bono?*, is strictly distinguished from murder, *lifut,* which is killing without any such reason. Bono? is feared and considered wrong, but it is recognized as a dangerous possibility, a potential explosion of moral outrage in search of re-taliation. One can only hold so much before his self-esteem and his standing require some vindication. Should a foolish person lower a man's standing—should he challenge his very manhood, for ex-ample, by making love to his wife—he has, in a sense, called that man's standing into public question. Were the man to do nothing in return, he would accept that lower standing. A bad fedew wants to purge the pain, assuage the anger, and seek vindication. One such way—extreme and wrong to Tiruray, but completely understand-able to them—is to kill.

Sigayan, speaking of Awang Tiruray custom as he knew it in the mid-nineteenth century, gives this description of revenge killing:

> Now the way they kill, if there is somebody with whom they are angry or against whom they have a grudge, is this: they go after revenge. When it is still daytime, they set out hiking to the place of the one they hate. Then, when they are at that place, and it is night, they shoot him with their bow and arrow, or else they might spear him as he sleeps. The revengers hide, for they do this killing with stealth. Once they have killed, they move away a bit—but they do not proceed home. They stay near the one whom they stabbed, in order to make sure from the sounds in the house whether the man died or not. When

they hear someone shout out "Who stabbed?" they, still being close by, will reply, "We did; we came on behalf of . . . ,
our friend." After that the killers go home, for they are satisfied.[5]

Mo?ensay, an elderly kefeduwan now living beyond the Tran in
the Basak homesteading area who frequently returns to his old
haunts near Figel and the traditional tribal atmosphere which he
finds vastly more congenial, told me this story, so similar in detail
to Sigayan's:

> He said that before the coming of the Japanese [the great
> chronological bench mark of recent times, he probably means
> the thirties, but possibly the twenties] his aunt, ?Amuŋ, was
> caught by her husband, Liwas, having sexual intercourse with
> Samberan, a cousin of Liwas. The infuriated husband lunged
> at them with his field knife, but there was much scrambling
> about and confusion, and the illicit lovers were able to run
> away. Liwas reported what had happened to his uncle, who
> was an important kefeduwan and the leader of his family and
> who was known by the title Datu Kafitan. He sent messengers
> at once to call for the principal elders closely related to ?Amuŋ,
> two kefeduwan, named Minted and Masela?. They arrived
> within several hours, and asked to settle the case nicely—agree-
> ing that ?Amuŋ had the sala? (the fault of Samberan, at this
> point, not being their concern) and offering to return the en-
> tire brideprice. Datu Kafitan could not locate Liwas, however.
> Later that night, four men—Liwas and three relatives—ap-
> peared at the place of ?Amuŋ's parents and, with a bolo, re-
> peatedly stabbed ?Amuŋ's father through the slat floor of his
> elevated house. He was dead within a few hours. In the morn-
> ing, when Masela? and Minted arrived, and when they learned
> that Liwas had taken blood revenge for his bad fedew, they
> called together all of the close kinsmen of ?Amuŋ's father.
> Some were told to proceed with the burial, but most prepared
> to revenge his death. The same day a large group left to bono?.

5. Tenorio (1892:33,34). The translation is mine and is taken from the
Tiruray text. Bennasar's Spanish translation is not always faithful to the
original and must be used with caution.

That night they slept by the river, near the settlement of Liwas, and early in the morning they ambushed Bilu? and Buluntu?, two first cousins of Liwas, who had gone to gather bamboo. Both were killed. Datu Kafitan called for Masela? and Minted to come and adjudicate the matter before there was more loss of life, and it was settled without any further killing.

Another well remembered example:

He [a middle-aged man] said that his grandfather had gone to bono? as a young man, when his older brother's wife had eloped with a man from beyond Bantek [in the mountains about 15 kilometers south of Upi]. His grandfather's brother was very hot and called his relatives together, saying that they should go at once to seek blood revenge. A large group went to the place of the eloper, where they killed five of his close relatives. Nothing more happened for over a year, and then the men of that place came and killed almost twenty of his grandparent's kindred.

Several salient features of revenge killing appear in these accounts which contribute to its bloody and disruptive character and therefore to the general fear in which it is held in this society. Bono? is usually by stealth, striking without warning, which necessitates an extreme and often long-lasting vigilance. It spreads beyond the exact individuals involved in the original 'foolish' act to endanger entire kindreds, and it rapidly escalates from a single act of revenge into a widening and self-perpetuating feud.

Tales tell of fabulously brave ?alek, 'heroes,' who, fearing no man, would seek revenge openly. Instead of stabbing his opponent through the floor of his house or falling upon him by ambush, a 'hero' would place two stakes along a trail he knew the opponent would pass, marking off an area in which they would fight. Seeing this warning, the person could draw his kris and prepare to defend himself before entering the area. When fully ready to fight, he would spring into the marked-off stretch of trail, shouting "Who is challenging me?" at which time the revenger would come from his hiding place. This way of challenging openly is called 'cutting short one's hiding' (*kemereb fera$^{\gamma}$a$^{\gamma}$*) and is said to be rare—characteristic of heroes but not of ordinary men and ordinary revenge. Usually, as in the stories told above, the revenge is 'hidden' (*mono$^{\gamma}$ seniruŋ*) and thus is an effective leveler—the famous fighter is no more frightening when he seeks revenge than is any other man. So long as there is the possibility that someone may have a hating fedew toward an individual, the individual must fear the sudden arrows from along the path, a sudden spear thrust through the floor when he is asleep, the blast of a homemade shotgun fired from concealment. Sharpened spurs of bamboo must be set into the ground all around the home. Watchfulness and care must be constant; life is reduced to siege.

Not only is the offender himself thrown into danger and fear, but anyone in his entire kindred is apt to be killed in revenge for what he did. The responsibility (sala$^{\gamma}$) is borne by all close relatives of the actual one responsible (the mensala$^{\gamma}$) for the bad fedew. One of the most immediate and most vexed rebukes that an offending individual can expect from his elders is that he has placed his relatives in grave danger. From the time the wrong is committed until it is settled by successful adjudication, there is anxiety among all the close kinsmen. Similarly, any close relative of the one hurt and craving vindication is likely to share in his sense of pain and benal and may well join him in a revenge killing raid.

Killing in revenge leads to further killing in counterrevenge. However human and understandable it may be in the Tiruray scheme, it is still wrong to them; it causes bad fedew, and it establishes new threats. Even though the one killed in revenge may have precipitated his own death by foolishly hurting someone's fedew—even though he clearly had the fault (sala$^{\gamma}$)—still his relatives will be expected to avenge him. Thus vengeance turns into feuding, not only extending outward to include the full kindreds of each person involved, but perpetuating itself forward in time as each killing to satisfy honor creates a new expectation for killing in return.

The explosion of a hurt fedew into bono$^{\gamma}$ may be instantaneous if the offender is at hand, as when Liwas found his wife $^{\gamma}$Amuŋ in the act of cuckolding him with Samberan and (albeit unsuccessfully) tried to stab them both on the spot.

I caught a ride with the mayor in his jeep and learned of a bonoʔ killing that had occurred a few weeks ago in Mangga. The son of Moŋgoʔ of that place had run away with the wife of Serumfoŋ of Benuan, near Kuya. The trouble was settled by adjudication, but Moŋgoʔ did not send the peace offering when he was supposed to, so Serumfoŋ went to his house to get it. While they were eating, Moŋgoʔ began to grossly insult Serumfoŋ who is a short fellow with only stumps of fingers on one hand as a result of leprosy years ago. Moŋgoʔ said that he was deformed and small, that he doubted that he need even bother giving such a cripple a peace offering, that he doubted that he could kill if he wanted to. Serumfoŋ said nothing, but continued eating and tried to hold his anger. Moŋgoʔ got a homemade shotgun and rudely threw it at Serumfoŋ saying, "Here, here is your peace offering." Serumfoŋ apparently ignored the taunt and just placed the gun on his lap and went on eating. Unseen, however, he slipped in a shell, and when Moŋgoʔ insulted him again he shot him, blowing him to bits with a 12-gauge shell at close range. Then he ran away, and turned himself in to the mayor at Nuro. The mayor said that he had called for the relatives from both sides and had been promised that the matter would be settled without further bloodshed. Moŋgoʔ's brother (an important kefeduwan) had investigated the situation and had accepted that his brother had been gravely at fault; he had agreed to settle the matter to the satisfaction of all by way of tiyawan.

In this case, bonoʔ had not drawn the kindred of the one upon whom vengeance had been taken into counterrevenge and feuding; rather, cooler heads had prevailed, and the issues involved had been submitted to adjudication. This is the third of the major responses to a hurt fedew, and the moral response to a desire for retaliation (benal). If one cannot hold until the anger seeps away, but feels that his fedew must have some acceptable recompense for what it has suffered, he should still settle the issue in the fatut way—he should inform the kefeduwan, so that in tiyawan they might decide the fault (salaʔ) and the proper restitution (benal) officially, assess the appropriate fines, and thus restore his good fedew. Formal adjudication, tiyawan, is a deeply serious matter and the context of

the distinctive form of leadership among the Tiruray. Just as morality is the society's primary defense against the ravages of a bad
fedew, so tiyawan are the final line of defense against the outbreak
of violence.

Tiruray moral ideas define what, for them, is good, and they
guide behavior that, for them, is right. Similarly, they define what
is bad and identify conduct that is wrong and 'foolish.' They establish an ultimate moral standard—respect—and they tie it to a
pervasive moral symbol, the fedew. They set forth the responsibility
of the wrongdoer for the consequences of his disrespect, stressing
that human nature is such that the consequences could be bloody,
indeed. They institutionalize the obligation of respect into specific
customs and into a general, variable standard: the ?adat, in both of
its senses. It is in terms of these ideas that the Tiruray attempts to
behave in a respectful and responsible manner.

All of this seeks to work out in practice the normative aspects of
Tiruray common sense, which constitute the imperatives of Tiruray
morality. Throughout, however, it is clear that this moral code suf-
fers from the limitations which are generic to moral systems.

The first inherent difficulty of moral systems derives from the
diffuse sources of the social pressure which support moral obligations and render them difficult and inefficient to maintain.[6] A system of straightforward moral imperatives and prescriptions making
up the oughts for social life is, by itself, poorly equipped to deal
with real or supposed breaches of the standards. For example, a
person ought not to steal the rice from your granary, and yet you
return home to find that someone has helped himself. What follows?
Is it now proper for you to steal some rice back from the one you
know—or think you know—did it? Suppose the individual you
"know" to have done it denies that he did; how do you know that
you know? Granted some clear moral obligation (not to steal) and
granted some clear violation (something was stolen), the inefficiency problem inherent in any moral system is that collective
morality, individually applied, cannot establish with authority either

6. This discussion of the difficulties inherent in the operation of a morality
derives from Hart's analysis of the "defects" in any regime of primary rules
alone. See Hart (1961:89 ff.).

what happened or what should be done. Such pressing issues as determination of the offender, of the punishment due him, of how it should be administered, of the satisfaction due the offended, and of how it should be claimed are left to the individuals involved and whatever support they can muster to their points of view. Suppose someone does not respect his companion's personal aversion (his keʔikaʔan), perhaps by foolishly mentioning the name of some individual for whom his companion has a deep hatred. What precisely is the proper satisfaction of his angered companion's fedew? Surely this is not sufficient grounds for a bloody feud. Morality recognizes a desire for restitution, that is, it recognizes benal; but benal to do what?

A second generic difficulty in moral systems springs from the general nature of moral obligations. They are not specific to certain individuals in certain situations, but rather refer to classes of acts and classes of persons; their application necessarily requires that specific cases be identifiable as particular instances of general classes. Sometimes this is quite simple. A thief, sneaking in from another village with intent to rob a granary, looking furtively about, selecting a dark night when the owner is away, and so forth, is an instance of stealing, a plain and clear case of the general concept. But, along with a core of settled meaning, there is in every general concept a more blurred, fuzzy edge where some of the features of the classic core case are present but others are either not there or are different. You were gone, and someone took the grain without asking because he needed it right then; he had planned to ask you, had you been home. Did he steal it or did he borrow it? The issue here is not the same as in the first case discussed. It is not "Is X the one who stole?" or "What should be done with X in view of his being a thief?" It is rather the very different question, "Is what X did to be considered stealing?" One ought not wantonly endanger another's life. But, when the youth from Tuwol tested out his home-made shotgun, not knowing that Mosew was walking nearby in the cool of the evening, was his act—however unintentional—sufficiently imprudent to constitute 'foolishness'? Was it simply an unfortunate accident and a narrow escape for Mosew, or did the boy wrong him? A moral standard cannot, itself, determine whether it

is applicable to a particular act. It can only direct the determining
individuals to its unambiguous core examples; the individual must
himself then classify it as falling under the standard or not, according to his interpretation and assessment of the resemblances
and the variations he takes to be critical.[7]

Still a third problem arises in trying to live according to a system
of morality. Moral standards are part of a culture's view of reality;
they are taken for granted as being rooted in the very nature of the
world itself, and thus as being inherently immune to conscious
human modification. Received moralities are felt to be eternal veri-
ties, which means that they find change difficult to incorporate.
There is no way to introduce a new moral rule, however needed;
no authoritative procedure is felt competent to eliminate an existing
moral rule, however dysfunctional it may have become. Both situations defy the logic of the givenness of moral obligations. A man,
for example, should not scold another man, unless they are closely
related, for it will constitute, to Tiruray, despising. But, suppose
the first person has become a municipal policeman and he has
spoken concerning the breaking of a law. Tiruray custom knows
nothing of municipal police forces or of Philippine laws. Do these
new things in Tiruray life alter the obligation of the Tiruray policeman not to interfere in the schemes and activities of another man
—for surely that is the rule of custom? The oughts are seen by
participants in a morality as facts of life, inexorable and unalterable. The idea of a "new morality" is invariably offensive and
threatening to those whose common sense incorporates an older
system.

These three difficulties in living according to a conventional
morality—the maintenance inefficiency, the generality, and the unalterability of moral obligations—comprise a set of cultural strains
inherent in any moral system per se.[8] In this sense, the difficulties
may be viewed as tending toward law. In any society they call for
the establishment of a certain set of sociocultural institutions to

7. The literature on the problem of the general and the particular is, of
course, immense. For discussions of the problem as it applies directly to
moral and legal reasoning, see Hart (1961:121 ff.), Stone (1961:137 ff.).
8. The idea of "cultural strains" is taken from Geertz; see (1964:64).

serve as practical and adaptive elaborations upon the moral bare
bones of normative common sense. These are the legal institutions
of a society.

The problem of generality—whether in a particular case a particular obligation did or did not exist—may result, in one society,
in authoritative reference to a set of statutes and, in another society,
in autonomic ordeals. Maintenance inefficiency may be dealt with
among one people by investing their chiefs with absolute adjudicatory authority and punitive power, among others by the development of a complex system of courts and prisons. The unalterability
of moral obligation may underlie the emergence of institutions as
substantively different as a legislature and an infallible papacy. The
problems and their attendant strain toward institutional elaboration
are generic; the substantive content of resulting ideas and structures
is not.

Institutionalized in different ways in different societies, and internalized to varying degrees in various individuals within any specific society, "the legal" may thus be seen as being related to and
emerging from a matrix of "the moral" in the occurrence of this
particular cluster of cultural responses.

The rest of this study will describe the legal institutions in Tiruray life which exist to deal authoritatively with precisely such difficulties in the recognition and observance of moral demands.

Chapter 3   The Kefeduwan
                               and the Tiyawan

ONE OF the important specialized roles in Tiruray life is that of the legal authority, the kefeduwan. This man is a moral leader, as is any Tiruray elder among his kin juniors, but he has the particular specialty of being one of a fraternity of legal representatives and experts. His work as kefeduwan, as I have mentioned, is conducted in tiyawan, the formal adjudicatory discussion in which he and his colleagues manifest the expertise in Tiruray custom and law which constitutes their distinctive specialization. The tiyawan is the setting for the formal negotiation of agreements, of which marriage is the most common and serious example, and for the nonviolent settlement of disputes.

The role of kefeduwan is not tied to wealth, as there is virtually no such differentiation among traditional Tiruray. Nor can it be called a profession, as kefeduwan carry on the same subsistence activities as all other men. They farm their swiddens and help in their neighbors' fields. They hunt, fish, and gather wild foods in the forest as do those who are not kefeduwan. The distinguishing capacity of the kefeduwan is his ability to participate actively in the discussion at a tiyawan. Any person who learns to speak in the highly metaphorical rhetoric of a tiyawan and who is accepted by his companions as a trustworthy representative in the work accomplished by tiyawan will be known as a kefeduwan.[1]

Mosantos [a middle-aged man of Figel] told me this morning that he thought the three most important characteristics of a good kefeduwan were that he have a cool head, that he know how to think, and that he have a fantastic memory. He said that because Bala?ud was so renowned for these attributes, he was the greatest of all the Tran kefeduwan.

Any Tiruray would concur. It is of prime importance that a kefeduwan be able to endure the most heated discussion without showing anger. Tiyawan deal with matters of the gravest importance and stand as the primary Tiruray alternative to bloody feuding. In such circumstances, anyone who would participate in an effort to "settle it nicely" must keep a cool head himself and must be adept at reasoning with others in a way that calms rather than inflames.

By his reference to knowing how to think, Mosantos was referring to a cluster of important characteristics. The kefeduwan must be thoroughly familiar with the smallest details of Tiruray custom. He must know not only the rules of respect that constitute one great body of custom, but he must also be able to reason clearly and convincingly about whether this or that action was consistent with proper interpersonal relations, with the general proscription against any action that violates decent respect for the fedew of other individuals. He must, moreover, be intimately acquainted with the more specialized customs concerning tiyawan: how they proceed, what consequences flow from what decisions, and so forth. In general, he must know well the customs governing kefeduwan behavior as such.

The fantastic memory alluded to is certainly one of the most spectacular of kefeduwan attributes. I have witnessed time and again the ability of a kefeduwan to recite the precise composition of a brideprice settlement—how many of this tamuk item and how many of that, what was given by the time of the wedding and what was

1. Of the twenty-nine male heads of families in Figel neighborhood, two are considered to be major kefeduwan and seven to be minor kefeduwan.

given later, a physical description of the size and characteristics of each kris and each brass betel quid box—and all of this twenty or thirty years after the settlement was accomplished! Traditional Tiruray are, of course, illiterate; no written records exist of tiyawan transactions. But detailed records do exist in the memories of any participating kefeduwan. Impressive to witness in action, the memory of an able kefeduwan for details of past settlements is crucial to his work.

Much the same general criteria for a promising kefeduwan appear in the following passage, along with three additional ones:

> Mo?inugal [a Figel neighborhood kefeduwan] and I spoke for a while about Moligaya [another Figel man, who was beginning to speak during tiyawan and was considered as a potential kefeduwan]. Mo?inugal said that he thought Moligaya would become a great kefeduwan in time. He can speak well in metaphors and euphemy and goes right to clear points, so that other kefeduwan feel in agreement with him. He has done many foolish things such as frequently grabbing other men's wives, but from that experience he has become well familiar with the details of the ?adat for settling troubles. Moreover, he has an excellent memory for past tiyawan. Given many alternatives, Mo?inugal said, a good kefeduwan must be able to weigh the advantages and disadvantages of each possible decision, recognize the most just alternative, and be able to reach a decision. Moligaya, he felt, was very decisive in just that way. Moreover, Moligaya is not afraid to part with tamuk and is willing to see his own tamuk used to make peace. He is willing to give up tamuk if it will help make a fedew good, even though he has no fault. Most important of all, he is most concerned that the rights of all persons be fairly treated, whoever they may be—whether his own kinsmen or not. He wants every fedew to be good.

It is considered fitting for a kefeduwan to demonstrate a very great level of generosity with regard to tamuk. In a tiyawan regarding fault, the fine is not paid by the one directly at fault, but by his kefeduwan. A readiness to part with tamuk is, therefore, essential to the kefeduwan role as it is meant to operate. Not all kefeduwan display this attribute, to be sure, but those who lack it are not given much respect.

> Many speak ill of [a local kefeduwan who is not trusted] and say that his main interest in a tiyawan is to get tamuk that he can sell for pesos. They say nobody approves of his way and they don't know any other kefeduwan that would do what he does. One old woman told me, "A kefeduwan should work hard in his fields, just like everyone else. Tiyawan are not to earn, but to help. A kefeduwan who gets tamuk should not sell it. He should hold on to it to help his people when they have to give."

Being concerned primarily with the rights and feelings of all involved people and aiming at the goal of everyone's having a good fedew go to the heart of the Tiruray concept of justice. Kefeduwan represent a particular person—more accurately, a particular person and his kindred—but they do not contend in the manner of trial lawyers in adversary proceedings. They do not try to win for their side. Together, all kefeduwan participating in a tiyawan are expected to strive earnestly to achieve a situation where all benal has been recognized, where those responsible for the trouble have—through their kefeduwan—accepted their responsibility and fault and have been properly fined, so that all fedew have been made good (fiyo). Kefeduwan act much more like a fraternity of judges than like an array of lawyers; they are committed as a group to an ultimate respect for just decisions, decisions that set every fedew right. Among kefeduwan this commitment is all-important.

A kefeduwan that seems to contend for his own party in a tiyawan is severely censured and is said to be a *lemiful* ('cheating') kefeduwan. Such a person is not respected by his fellow kefeduwan and is not asked by his own relatives to "care for their fedew." Another form of 'cheating' consists of a kefeduwan's never appearing when there is a fault to accept and tamuk to be given as a fine. A kefeduwan who cheats in this way is likely to turn up to discuss the brideprice at a tiyawan where he is in the kindred of the girl and thus will receive some of the brideprice tamuk. But he is nowhere to be found when he is in the kindred of the man and thus will have to give tamuk. This is 'cheating' behavior because it aims at getting tamuk rather than at achieving justice.

> He [an old man of Figel] said that, although Moʔaŋgul was a major kefeduwan and had been very famous in years past, now he was not respected, as he was always cheating. I asked him to tell me a few examples of Moʔaŋgul's cheating, and he told me that several months before, Mosew had asked Moʔaŋgul to help give tamuk for Mofasiyo, a nephew of his who was marrying a woman with whom he had eloped. Moʔaŋgul replied that he could not think about such things as his mind was now old and cloudy. A week later, however, Moʔaŋgul attended the brideprice negotiation tiyawan for the marriage of his niece and talked and talked. When it came to receiving tamuk his head was quite clear enough.

Because a kefeduwan is dedicated to seeing that all faults are properly accepted and rights properly respected—which to Tiruray *is* justice because it restores a situation where all fedew are good— it is quite permissible and common for a kefeduwan to take part in a tiyawan where he is equally related to both parties. Normally, this situation is considered especially desirable because the kefeduwan—called in such a case a *bito keraraʔ,* 'a woven basket in the middle'—is trusted equally by all concerned. My informant's second example of Moʔaŋgul's cheating ways, however, concerned a marriage tiyawan in which he was a bito keraraʔ:

> He said that when Mokediŋon and Liwanag were wedded, Moʔaŋgul was a basket in the middle, being related by blood to the man's side and by marriage to the woman's side. At the wedding, when it came to eating food rather than preparing it, he shouted loudly that he was a leader in the man's kindred; but at the tiyawan where the final amount of brideprice goods was given, he did more talking than anyone, always arguing from the point of view of the bride's party—clearly hoping to receive some of the brideprice when it was distributed.

A kefeduwan is said to be *tugiʔen,* 'lying,' if he makes promises and agreements in order only to conclude a tiyawan and then does not abide by the promises. Such a person is felt to be less interested in seeing that everybody's fedew is good, than merely in escaping trouble. Such a kefeduwan loses the respect of his fellow kefeduwan, and they will not engage in tiyawan with him if he is alone in representation of his party. The kefeduwan of the other party will insist that he have a companion they trust to join him in accepting fault or in making agreements.

When an individual wishes to make some formal agreement such as marriage between his kindred and someone else's, or when someone reports to his kefeduwan that he has a bad fedew which should go to tiyawan, the kefeduwan will contact an appropriate kefeduwan in the kindred of the other man, either by going to see him or by sending a messenger. A date is then set for the tiyawan, and each kefeduwan notifies the appropriate concerned individuals.

Individual Tiruray are said to be *kuyug*, 'followers,' of a certain kefeduwan. This does not mean that each legal leader has his specific, discrete following for whom he alone functions in tiyawan. A follower is said to 'trust his fedew' to a particular kefeduwan for a tiyawan. He may trust his fedew to several for a given tiyawan, or he may trust his fedew to different kefeduwan at one tiyawan than at another. One can, in traditional Tiruray society, decide whose follower one wishes to be, and it need not be a relative, though that is most common. The follower is then said to be within the *sakuf*, 'the area of [a certain kefeduwan's] authority.' Frequently a lesser kefeduwan will have a certain sakuf of followers, usually close relatives that live nearby. For these followers, the minor kefeduwan will speak in tiyawan that do not concern matters of very grave consequence. However, in more serious situations the lesser kefeduwan and his followers will all be followers of a major kefeduwan, to whom they will go to 'trust their fedew.' There are, thus, nesting circles of sakuf, within which people are related to various kefeduwan.

It should be stressed that this relationship does not involve political power. The concern of the kefeduwan is to stand for his follower in the making of contracts and in the settlement of troubles, his fundamental loyalty being not to the personal interests of his follower, but to the making of all things good, as manifested in the

good fedew of all persons concerned in the tiyawan. Although the
decisions of kefeduwan have authority, they cannot be backed by
force. Legal leaders among the traditional Tiruray are authoritative; they are not powerful. A decision that someone was at fault
and should be fined is made and accepted by men who are completely powerless to force acceptance of any decision. They cannot
have anyone beaten, ostracized, imprisoned in any sense, or exe-
cuted.

Beyond their ability to actually participate in tiyawan, kefeduwan
do not have a different status than nonkefeduwan. They farm and
hunt and fish along with their neighbors. A kefeduwan is generally
regarded as being wise, but not necessarily more so than a nonkefeduwan in matters that do not concern custom and tiyawan.

The tiyawan is actually a special kind of discussion. Tiruray use
a variety of terms to define different sorts of conversations between
people. The most broad term, sebereh, means simply 'talk together,'
in which the talk may or may not have any specific topic and the
participants may be any individuals. Sebereh is the general term for
people speaking to each other. One kind of sebereh, however,
se?urét?urét, may be glossed as 'discussing together'; when a group
se?urét?urét, their conversation has some definite topic. They are
not only talking; they are talking about something. The topic may
be anything at all—the weather, the best time for planting, some
story of the "old folks." A subtype of 'discussing together' is used
when the discussants are all kefeduwan and when the topic of the
discussion is some issue which requires decision. This kind of discussion is setiyawan, 'to adjudicate together,' and the conversation
itself is called a tiyawan, which may be glossed 'litigation.' Tiyawan
need not be concerned with a dispute; the discussion may be working out an agreement between two or more parties, but the intention
of kefeduwan when they setiyawan is always to resolve some issue
by arriving at an authoritative decision concerning it. While only
kefeduwan 'adjudicate together,' anyone may bring an issue to a
kefeduwan to be adjudicated.

Whether the concern of the tiyawan is an agreement or a dispute,
the authoritative decision reached is one in which all participating
kefeduwan concur. It is not the general Tiruray way for some spe-

cific individual to hand down an authoritative pronouncement. The latter rare situation, when it occurs, is called *kemukum,* 'to pronounce authoritative judgment' (a term derived from Arabic and borrowed from the Maguindanao *hukum,* 'to judge').

Tiyawan occur when they are needed; there is no set schedule for them. Word is sent around to concerned kefeduwan that there is to be a tiyawan at a certain place on a certain day, and all who are involved and others who wish to participate attend. Weddings are often the setting for numerous tiyawan, as they are the scene of large gatherings of kefeduwan—many of whom actually attended more for the anticipated tiyawan than for the wedding itself.

Following the marriage feast of Mokediŋon (an important kefeduwan from Tuwol, several kilometers upriver from Figel), there were five tiyawan, lasting some sixteen hours. The day of the wedding tiyawan itself began with that one at 8:15 A.M. and went on without a break until 7:30 P.M. The next day, they began again at 9:00 A.M. and adjudicated together until 1:15 P.M. Twelve kefeduwan attended, and all present participated to lesser or greater degree in all five tiyawan. Many had come expressly for the purpose of settling some matter in tiyawan rather than to witness Mokediŋon's marriage festival.

When the tiyawan concerns the negotiation of a marriage agreement, it always occurs at a place of the man's kindred, where the kindred of the intended bride goes, expecting to return home with tamuk. The tiyawan at the wedding itself is—like all weddings—at the bride's place. When a spouse has died, a tiyawan is conducted to settle matters of concern between the kindred to the deceased and that of his or her widow. This always occurs at the home of the dead and during the seventh-day activities, a time when the kindred of the deceased is invited to gather. Should a replacement spouse be agreed upon, there is a tiyawan for the giving of the additional tamuk; this is always held at the place of the new spouse, whichever sex it may be, with the widow or widower going to that place with his kindred, bearing tamuk, and returning home with a new spouse.

At a tiyawan, the kefeduwan all sit around in a rough circle on the floor. There is no set placement for any individual, and many who leave for a few moments to discuss something privately or to relieve their bladders return to different places than they had occupied previously. Those who represent the same party in the tiyawan need not sit beside each other or in any set location with regard to the kefeduwan from the other party. Kefeduwan sit in a traditional posture, with their legs crossed. Around them are placed their various betel quid needs, and each kefeduwan sets his kris on the floor at his side. This fighting sword and the fighting spear are generally carried by kefeduwan attending a tiyawan, particularly one concerning a dispute where the opposed parties are actually or technically enemies until the matter is settled.

Kefeduwan employ a highly metaphorical manner of speech when they adjudicate together, so that a nonkefeduwan is often puzzled as to the meaning of what he hears. The following bit of conversation between kefeduwan occurred when the man's side (A) arrived a day late for a marriage festival and found the woman's party (B) quite angry about the delay. The matter actually stopped short of tiyawan, but the conversation was conducted in the tiyawan rhetoric, called *binuwaya*ʔ:

B1: What is your purpose in coming here? Your place was perhaps the victim of earthquake and landslides; you are here looking for some place to live. (*The point*: What made you so late?)

B2: (*referring to the food prepared the preceding day*) You are welcome to eat here; I am only sorry that our food is all rotten and smelly. I don't know whether we can find good food or not. (*Point*: It is not certain whether the wedding will proceed.)

B1: It may be wasted; I don't know. My teeth are gone, and my eyes are bad. (*Point*: It is up to the others what will be done.)

B3: My fedew is bad. We have had much sickness here in this place, but still we tended our fires; no one should go about in an epidemic, but still we were busy. (*Point*: They had gone to much trouble to prepare for the wedding.)

A1: We too are not well. When I left yesterday to join my relatives before coming here, all in my place were sick,

even my wife. Therefore we were late, because we were all
sick. (*Point*: Illness is offered as an excuse for being late.)

A2: (*interrupting, not wanting a lying excuse to be made*) We
were mistaken in our days; can we not try your food? Let
us give you tamuk so that we can play music together on
our gongs. (*Point*: They were at fault and accept that;
may the wedding proceed?)

B2: (*accepting the apology and "dropping charges"*) It is all
as it should be with us. We have been sad because we are
in mourning for our ancestors, who cannot be here to enjoy our festivities.

B3: Yes, let us forget the delay and our sadness for the old
folks; let us proceed with our feast. You are all here now.

The ability to use and to understand this roundabout form of speaking characterizes a real kefeduwan. Things are not spoken of openly but are alluded to beneath the metaphors. Kefeduwan say that
this way of talking is used because it is extremely euphemistic and
thus is appropriate for discussing sensitive issues. Delicate matters
may be said this way which would hurt feelings if they were spoken
straight out. This is doubtless the main reason, through there is hardly any question that this rhetoric also serves to mark a kefeduwan
and that it is a source of pride and standing to excel at its use.

Learning to handle himself in the binuwaya? mode of conversation is one of the most critical skills that a man who would be a
kefeduwan must acquire. There is no formal rite of recognition of
a kefeduwan. Anyone may actually speak out in a tiyawan, whether
a kefeduwan or not, and often a layman sitting around listening
will venture an opinion in the discussion or tell something which he
thinks is pertinent to the tiyawan's concerns. When a nonkefeduwan
begins to take a greater and greater part in the discussion, when he
begins to demonstrate good judgment, a facile rhetoric, and a penetrating command of Tiruray custom, people will begin to listen very
attentively to him. In time, he may be asked by some close relative
to represent him in some minor matter that has come to tiyawan.
Once someone has trusted his fedew to the man and the fellow has
represented him in a tiyawan, however minor, people will consider
him to be a lesser kefeduwan. With time and practice, more and

more individuals may join his nascent following, and the individual has become a member of the informal but important fraternity of kefeduwan.

This group never meets as a formal body and does not constitute any kind of council, but together the kefeduwan may be considered to comprise the fundamental secular leadership of the traditional tribesmen and to stand at the pinnacle of public esteem. Tiruray exogamy rules and the propensity to marry women from far places means that throughout the Tiruray area there is a large network of kefeduwan who know each other and are accustomed to each other's ways. The larger integration of the society beyond neighborhoods is through this network and not through kinship (clans, etc.) or politics (chiefs, kings, etc.).

Tiruray divide tiyawan into two basic types: 'hot' (*meduf*) and 'good' (fiyo), and a kefeduwan must be able to negotiate in both. Those which result from a bad fedew situation are 'hot' tiyawan, which attempt to settle the bad fedew so that no one will be killed. In contrast, 'good' tiyawan are those in which no one is in danger. For example, a tiyawan to negotiate a marriage brideprice is not 'hot,' but 'good.' There is no bad fedew to be reckoned with—no need for any authoritative decisions regarding retribution or fault.

A 'good' tiyawan, of course, can turn 'hot.' Harsh or insulting words during a marriage arrangement tiyawan could turn a fedew bad and immediately raise the specter of bloodshed. In such circumstances the tiyawan would immediately become 'hot.' While such a transformation seldom occurs, a kefeduwan must be adept at handling both kinds of tiyawan.

Chapter 4   The Good Tiyawan

THE PROCESS of marriage establishment provides the principal occasions for good tiyawan. There are several ways of becoming *sebawag*, 'married'—by arrangement of elders or by elopement, for
example. But the most proper of the various methods of marriage-
making is called *segedot* and involves prior negotiations between
the kindred elders of the man and those of the woman.

It is important to keep in mind that, while a wedding unites a
man and a woman as spouses, the establishment of a marriage brings
into in-law relationship two kindreds: a *kelageyan*, 'the man's kindred,' and a *kelibunan*, 'the woman's kindred.' Most of the activities
connected with segedot concern the making of this in-law relationship between the kelageyan and the kelibunan. The wedding ceremony itself is merely a short episode in a long series of transactions.

Segedot involves three major steps: the establishment of the engagement between the two kindreds (*fetisiŋ*), a tiyawan for the negotiation and partial delivery of the brideprice (*seʔifar tamuk*), and
a marriage feast with tiyawan, at which the couple is wedded and
the remainder of the brideprice is given (*seferayan*).

Segedot is initiated by the elders of a man. When they determine
that they wish to arrange a marriage with a certain group on behalf
of their boy, his parents and perhaps an uncle go to the place of the

girl's parents. Along the way, they carefully watch for omens. Should they encounter a bad omen, like a bad bird call or some portent of death or other disaster, they turn back. If, however, they meet no bad omens along the way, they arrive—usually in the late morning —and euphemistically state their purpose. The roundabout announcement that they have in fact come to give a *tising,* 'betrothal offering' (two pieces of tamuk, like a kris and a necklace, which symbolize the desire for and acceptance of a formal engagement) allows the girl's parents an opportunity to refuse without risking the shame to the man's side which would come from a directly spoken refusal of a directly spoken offer of the betrothal offering.

> Tanigid of Mehengeb went to Tubak to give a betrothal offering to Moluwasan to create an engagement between his son and Moluwasan's daughter. When he and his wife arrived, Moluwasan greeted them and gave them coffee. Using a common expression signifying their desire to give the betrothal offering, Tanigid said, "We came here to look for a place to live near you." Moluwasan replied, "I'm sure that if you really want that, we can find a way for us all to be joined." Then the engagement was frankly and straightforwardly discussed.

Even after the subject has been broached frankly, the parents of the girl are free to accept or decline the betrothal offering. If they have already accepted one from some other family, that is reason enough, and the man's relatives will leave without feeling shamed. If the girl is still free from an engagement, but her parents do not wish to engage her to this particular man, they may offer some polite reason—she is still too young, she is sickly, or the like. In any case, if they do not accept an offered engagement, they present the relatives of the man forthwith with a piece of tamuk, called in this situation the *diruŋ mala,* 'to cover their shame.' It is understood that the diruŋ mala covers or eliminates any possibility that the man's relatives might feel that they had been shamefully treated. The diruŋ mala may be given in many different situations where there could be some question of public embarrassment. It openly recognizes the touchiness of a situation and signifies that no humiliation is intended. In accepting the diruŋ mala, the individual publicly expresses that no shame was felt.

If the parents of the girl accept the betrothal offering, they agree to the engagement of their daughter to the man, and the two kindreds of the couple are henceforth in a new relationship which leads, once the wedding occurs, to their being in-laws. As soon as the offering is accepted, the two sets of elders agree to a time for the seʔifar tamuk, 'passing-across of brideprice goods,' tiyawan. This tiyawan will precede the marriage feast by a short time and will be the occasion when the brideprice is negotiated.

Henceforth, until the couple is actually wedded, the parents of the girl keep the betrothal offering or give it over to the keeping of their kefeduwan. It is not to be used in the interim as tamuk or sold, as it technically remains the property of the boy's parents until the wedding, after which it belongs to the girl's kindred.

Once an engagement has been established by the acceptance of a betrothal offering, it is possible for either side to break it off, but the procedure is careful to ensure that possible shame is 'covered.' If the girl's side wishes to break off the engagement, they must return both pieces of tamuk in the betrothal offering plus an additional piece as diruŋ mala. If it is the boy's side that wishes to break off the relationship, they ask for the return of one piece, leaving the other as diruŋ mala.

The side breaking off the engagement must give an explanation, of course, and, whatever the actual reason may be, the explanation is always that there were bad omens. The boy's side will "have its bad omen" supposedly en route to the seʔifar tamuk at the home of the girl's kefeduwan; the girl's side will claim to have any bad omens also when they are on the way to that house. In either case, only the father proceeds, and, at the tiyawan, instead of arranging the brideprice he arranges the giving of the diruŋ mala.

The engagement of [Tanigid's son] and [Moluwasan's daughter] was broken off a week after the betrothal offering had been accepted. Moluwasan's younger brother, a kefeduwan named Mosiŋuwan, went to Tanigid and told him that they had had

a bad omen. In fact, what had happened was that when Moluwasan had informed his son's kindred of the engagement, they
told him what he had not known: long ago their ancestors had
had a bloody feud with Tanigid's forefathers. Mosiŋuwan felt
that although no grudge remained it was still imprudent to
have the two groups become in-laws. Therefore he went to
return the betrothal offering and to give a diruŋ mala.

In the morning, as the relatives of the man are gathering at the
house, and as some additional relatives of the girl may also be arriving, there is a general discussion of the omens that have been
observed. When all are present, the tiyawan itself begins. The kefeduwan and critical elders of the couple, naturally including their
parents, sit in a rough circle on the floor with the others standing,
squatting, or sitting around them. People not actually involved in
the talking mill about considerably. The kefeduwan themselves frequently shift position, leave to urinate or to discuss some point
privately with a companion from the same party, call for a betel
quid to be prepared for them by a wife, or bend low over a crack
in the bamboo slat floor to spit.

Talking at a seʔifar tamuk is only partially in roundabout tiyawan
style, as the immediate elders of the bride—who may or may not be
kefeduwan—have much to say and as most of the negotiating concerns concrete amounts of tamuk being asked for the various component parts of the felasaʔ, 'brideprice.' The woman's party begins
by stating forthrightly the total amount of goods that it wants in
each part.

The first component of the brideprice to be set consists of three
items, traditionally named the setuŋoran (literally, 'location where
the exchange occurs'), the tabid (literally, 'strands twisted together'), and the ʔofoʔ seʔifaran (literally, 'eldest sibling of that given').
These are necklaces of decreasing size, supposedly equal in cash
value to 120, 80, and 60 pesos, although in areas where plow farming has begun to replace swidden agriculture to any extent, the
setuŋoran asked might well be a carabao rather than a large necklace.

The setuŋoran, the tabid, and the ʔofo seʔifaran are, like some
other tamuk items and rituals that occur at the feast, given express-

ly in token of the fact that the bride-to-be is a maiden who has not been previously married, a *kenogon*. This is usually the case in segedot marriage arrangements. Should the woman not be a kenogon (if she is separated from a previous husband or if the brideprice is being negotiated for a woman who, being married, has run away with her present man), the man's side need not give any of the three. It might, however, agree to allow the woman's kindred, under such circumstances, to *fekenogon* their girl. This means literally to 'make a kenogon' of her by giving the man's side an item of tamuk, usually a large necklace or an especially handsome kris. To do so is considered an act of kindness by the man's side, for, while they thereby have the added pleasure and honor of getting a "maiden" for their boy, the fiction requires them accordingly to give the setuŋoran, the tabid, and the ʔofoʔ seʔifaran. The tamuk item used to restore maiden status to the bride-to-be is called a *fegefekenogon*, literally, 'that which is employed to make one be a kenogon'; being given by the woman's kindred to the man's side, it is not part of the brideprice itself.

When the woman's side has stated what it wants for the above three items, the next part of the brideprice to be discussed is the *ʔayam,* 'animals.' Before carabao came to be important among the peasantized Tiruray, animals were of considerably less value as brideprice items. If any animals were asked at all (many families did not, and some still do not, ask animals) they were usually horses, which were valued for travel along mountain trails and for certain methods of deer-hunting. In recent years, the value of carabao among peasantized Tiruray has become great, and the practice of asking for them has spread widely.

If animals are asked, they may be any number, at the discretion of the woman's side. Six, eight, and ten are commonly asked, although as few as two or as many as twenty appear in my tiyawan records. As in other circumstances involving numbers, Tiruray customarily ask for an even number, odd lots being considered incomplete and hence unlucky.

However many animals are asked by the woman's side, it is always understood that an equal number of tamuk items will accompany the animals, these being called the *lagaʔ*, the 'equivalent worth' of the animals. The tiyawan will discuss what items the woman's side wishes to have as laga?, although the number is predetermined by the number of carabao or horses.

The third part of the brideprice to be discussed is the necklaces. Again, the girl's side states how many necklaces they wish to receive in the settlement. Twenty or so is a common request, although there are instances when as many as forty are asked.

The final part of all brideprice settlements consists of items of tamuk that are named for steps in the ritual of the wedding feast; they are named after the steps with which they are associated. With one exception, these are of traditional size and character and need not be discussed specifically in the negotiation of the brideprice. The exception is the *saran,* 'place to sit,' which varies in amount according to how fancy a bench the woman's side intends to prepare for the groom to sit on when he first arrives at the wedding feast. The saran may be from one to several pieces of tamuk, or, as is increasingly common today, may be asked in terms of money, perhaps five or ten pesos.

If the bride-to-be is not only a maiden (a real one) but is also the last or only daughter of her parents, seven additional items of tamuk are included in the brideprice. These need not be discussed, as they are always the same traditional items. The pieces are named after things which were used at the birth of the bride and immediately afterward: the *?enos,* 'cloth for wiping the newborn child,' always one sarong; the *keraraw,* 'basin,' always a large gong; the *fuyul?on,* 'cradle,' always one sarong; the *taley,* 'cradle rope,' always one necklace; the *kifen,* 'cradle support,' always one kris; the *gut-gut,* 'to rock,' always one necklace; and the *fuyu?,* 'cradle spring stick,' which is always one spear.

Another item of tamuk which is part of a brideprice only under certain circumstances is the *lentu?,* 'leap over.' Tiruray sisters properly are wedded in order of birth. The lentu? is one item of tamuk— for example, a kris or a spear—which is given only if the bride-to-be has an older sister who is still unmarried; one lentu? is given for each such sister. Lentu? and the seven pieces mentioned above, if they apply, are supposed to be given at the time of the formal negotiation of the brideprice.

One last item should be mentioned, although it is not actually part of the brideprice. Should the couple to be wedded be consanguineal third cousins, it is necessary for the two sides to exchange single pieces of tamuk called *fegesederi*ʔ, 'to push them apart,' so that the union will not be considered incestuous. The exchange of these items must occur before any other discussion of the brideprice can take place.

When the woman's side has stated the entire brideprice it is asking, the man's kindred representatives must decide and announce whether they feel that they can give it or not. It is not necessary that the entire amount be given on the spot—although it could be, and it would be to the credit of the man's side should they be so well prepared. If the man's kindred decides that it cannot ever hope to give the brideprice asked, it gives one piece of tamuk to the girl's side to cover any shame and goes home. The tiyawan is over, and the engagement is no longer in effect.

If, on the other hand, the man's side agrees to the brideprice stated—as is usual—they then state how much must be *bara*ʔ, 'unpaid balance,' until the marriage feast. In practice, it is tacitly understood that even after the marriage feast tiyawan some balance will probably remain unpaid. Should the woman's kindred not be willing to allow the requested amount of unpaid balance and the man's party not be able to reduce it, the woman's side returns the betrothal offering along with an item of tamuk to cover shame, and the negotiations cease.

If the woman's side agrees to the requested unpaid balance, the man's side promises to give it at the marriage feast, and the tiyawan discussion then turns to a part of the brideprice, the size of which is determined not by the woman's, but by the man's side. This is the *barandiya*ʔ, or 'plates'—a quantity of small Chinese saucers traditionally valued at ten centavos and now almost invariably given in pesos rather than saucers.

When the undelivered balance has been agreed upon, the man's side hands over all that is to be given at once, and the tiyawan concludes with consideration of the date and details of the marriage feast.

Collection of the tamuk by the man's side is informal. The father

of the boy to be wedded does not actually ask for tamuk help in so
many words, but simply spreads the word among his son's relatives
that he is to be married. All known relatives, even if they are not
strictly members of the boy's kindred, help if they feel able.

The brideprice received by the girl's side is widely shared among
her close relatives. Should it ever have to be returned—as, for example, if the girl elopes with some other man—each individual who
received an item of the tamuk would be responsible for the return
of an equivalent amount, though not necessarily the identical item.
Tamuk changes hands rather frequently, as it is received for various
reasons and given out for various reasons. Any given brideprice is
thus not a continuing aggregate of concrete tamuk items; it is a continuing stated amount which serves to link many people to a given
marriage and concern them with its good health.

Once the seʔifar tamuk tiyawan has set a date for the marriage
feast, both parties to the wedding are bound to keep that date.
Should either side wish to postpone—and both sides frequently do,
in order to have more time for the preparations—then custom requires that a gift be given. If the woman's side wishes more time for
preparing the feast food, they send a messenger to the father of the
groom with a small bag of rice and one chicken. If the man's side
wishes more time to gather up the tamuk for the brideprice, they
send one item of tamuk to the father of the bride. This item, usually
but not necessarily a necklace or a kris, is not reckoned as part of
the brideprice.

In the regular marriage (segedot) process, the wedding ceremony itself occurs during a seferayan, 'elaborate initial marriage
feast,' which is one of four kinds of marriage feast, all characterized
by the man's side's giving tamuk and in return being fed by the
woman's kindred. If there is need to hurry up the marriage, as when
the couple has been having illicit sexual relations and the girl is
pregnant, a much simplified version of the marriage feast may be
celebrated, which is called sefedurus. In this, the various ceremonies
are alluded to but not actually performed, the amount of tamuk
given may be small (the girl's father under the circumstances having
lost much of his leverage), and the meal served is much less fancy.
The sefeʔinum, 'elaborate final marriage feast,' does not occur at

the time of the wedding, but if and when the man's side finally gives the last of the items in the brideprice. *Setebuh* is the fourth of the types of marriage feasts, and it is the smallest affair of them all, concerning only the married couple and the parents of the wife. It occurs shortly after the birth of each child and consists of the woman's parents' bringing food to the home of their son-in-law to welcome the newborn and receiving in return a traditional group of tamuk items.

On the day before the seferayan (elaborate initial marriage feast), the kindred of the girl gathers at the place of the feast, usually the big house of their major kefeduwan. The girl herself is still quite unaware that she is the one to be wedded and will believe that she is keeping the secret from some sister or cousin. In the early evening after eating, the people will all be chatting when the kefeduwan suddenly announces in a loud voice, "Now so-and-so (the girl) will be married to so-and-so (the boy)." Invariably, the girl begins to cry from embarrassment and to struggle to run away. As she is being held, all of her relatives present cry out four times in a traditional wedding cheer: *ʔu ʔu fri.* The maiden is then covered completely with a *rekeruŋ*, a handsome silk sarong, and, when her worst crying has subsided, she is placed in the house's *sibey,* an enclosed room where the maiden daughters of the kefeduwan or of any of his guests sleep at night. Several of her young unmarried girl friends stay with her, as do some older women to assure that she does not run away. The girl remains there, covered from head to foot in the silk sarong, until the following day when she is brought out for the actual wedding ceremony. In the sibey, the girl will not talk or allow her head to emerge from the sarong; she is only permitted to leave the room, with guards, to relieve herself. This procedure of announcing the girl's impending marriage is called *sesunur,* 'to inform.'

On the same day, the kindred of the groom-to-be has also gathered at the large house of their kefeduwan, and in the evening they surprise him with the same sesunur procedure. As the relatives all shout *ʔu ʔu fri* four times, the struggling of the young man is very great, and many men are required to hold him down and disarm him of his kris. He is also covered with a particularly handsome

sarong, and, although he is not placed in any special room, he is
guarded to ensure that he does not run away. Like the girl, the boy
is embarrassed and will not talk to anyone, keeping himself hidden
within the folds of the sarong for the rest of the evening. The following morning, he folds the sarong neatly and wears it across his
left shoulder from then on throughout the ensuing feast and wedding ceremony. Upon reaching home, the sarong will be given to
his bride.

On the morning of the feast, before leaving for the bride's place,
the man's side must prepare a *dudum,* 'canopy.' They get four poles
of round wood or bamboo and join them to form a rectangle with
pole framing at the top. This is covered with store-bought cloth,
which hangs down about one meter all the way around. At each
corner, the poles extending above the canopy are decorated with
banners. As the canopy will be given ultimately to someone on the
girl's side, it is a mark of generosity if the man's party uses fighting
spears as poles, instead of mere wood or bamboo. Before starting
for the feast, the man's side also confers informally among themselves to determine how much tamuk they are preparing to give at
the marriage feast tiyawan and who will give what at the various
places in the marriage feast ceremony where tamuk items are given.

At the place of the feast, the bride's kindred is busy preparing
many things on the morning of the celebration. A rail barrier, the
ʔalaŋ, is built on the path the man's group will arrive on. Made of
a simple pole of bamboo laid across two posts, the barrier cannot
be passed by the wedding party until someone in the man's party
has given the builder an item of tamuk (always a kris) which is
itself named "the ʔalaŋ."

Other men erect a *saran,* 'place to sit' (traditionally a bench with
a backrest) in the cleared area just in front of the big house. After
passing the ceremonial barrier, the groom will proceed to this bench
where, once a member of his party has given the builder a piece of
tamuk also named for this purpose "the saran," he sits down still
covered by his canopy.

Women of the girl's kindred cook great quantities of rice, wrap-
ping it into banana leaves in portions big enough for one meal. Five
of these *tenaley,* 'wrapped packets,' of rice are placed in a small

bark container along with an additional wrapped package containing one cooked chicken. The number of bark containers which must be prepared has been determined at the brideprice negotiation tiyawan when the man's side estimated how many of its families would be attending the marriage feast.

In addition to the bark containers of rice and chicken which will be given the man's party, the woman's side prepares three different kinds of special containers of food, the latter containers to be purchased by the groom's party at very high prices. A number of bride's women will prepare *benitin,* small woven bags filled with uncooked rice and hung on the rafters. With each of these, a live chicken is put aside. Any who wish may also prepare *sabakan,* funnel-shaped tubes of split bamboo into which have been placed five packets of cooked rice, one packet of cooked chicken, and a large bamboo internode of broth. The third specialty is a *maligey,* a decorated box hung, like the others, from the rafters and filled with such goodies from the coastal stores as rice cakes, coconut candy, cigarettes, and matches, as well as rice and chicken. At a typical elaborate marriage feast there may be as many as fifty benitin, each selling for a blouse and a sarong, four sabakan at fifteen pesos or the equivalent, and two maligey bringing twenty or twenty-five pesos each.

While the number of benitin, sabakan, and maligey is set in advance by the man's side, who will have to purchase them all at a dear price, the bride's party prepares any amount they desire of *dagaŋan,* 'sundries.' Various households set up little shoplike areas where they display—again, at greatly inflated prices—such things as soap, rice cakes, coffee, candies, and combs. In the "old days" it is said that the sundries consisted only of prepared betel quids and sticky rice cooked in a thin bamboo internode. By the time the groom's party arrives, the place has begun to resemble a small market.

The man's kindred times its journey to the celebration in such a way as to arrive in the early evening, an hour or so before dark. As the group nears the settlement where the feast is to occur, they begin to play their gongs. Everyone is dressed in his or her very best clothes. As soon as they are within hearing of the big house, they will shout out *ʔu ʔu fri* four times, and those awaiting them within

the large house will respond with four *?u ?u fri*. Before he can be
seen by any of the girl's side, the groom enters the cover of his
canopy.

Hearing the groom's party approaching, the bride's kinsman
who made the ceremonial barrier goes to meet them there. The
kefeduwan of the man's group says, "What are you asking for this
barrier?" and someone in the group hands over one piece of tamuk
as specified (usually a kris). The rail is then broken and thrown
aside, and all proceed to the clearing before the big house where
the bench has been prepared and where a number of large mats
have been spread for the groom's party to sit upon. When all are
seated on the mats, the groom within his canopy goes to the bench,
and, as soon as the tamuk item named for the bench is handed over,
he sits down. The posts of the canopy are driven into the ground,
the canopy still enveloping the seated groom.

As the groom's party is seated before the house, some of the
sundries of various kinds are brought for them to purchase at very
high prices. The Tiruray gongs are played, and many from both
sides join in the dancing. After some time, the kefeduwan of the
girl's side, along with her mother and father, go to the canopy, look
at the groom within to formally assure themselves that he is the
correct man and then take down the canopy, which is given to the
maker of the bench.

With that, one of the man's group stands up and holds out a spear
which is the *kelid gedan*, 'to prepare the ladder'; someone from the
woman's side steps forward and takes it; and the whole group goes
up into the big house, where the rest of the celebration takes place.
The mats are respread, and all on both sides sit down. Presently,
the leaders of the groom's party inquire into the cost of the items
hanging along the rafters overhead. As each is purchased, it is cut
down.

At this point, the women close to the groom will go to the little
room (sibey) in order to look at the bride and formally note that
she is the right person. For this, they must give the guard of the
room an item of tamuk (usually a good sarong) called the *fegelaŋu*,
'in order to see.' While this looking at the bride and groom is essentially a formality and a part of the general ceremony of the marriage

feast, there are tales of old times that tell of finding some other substituted woman, an outrage that is said at once to have resulted in a fierce hot tiyawan!

When at least one item has been cut down from the rafters, the meal itself begins. The girl's side places all of the bark containers of rice and chicken in front of the father of the groom, who distributes them to his kinsmen. When the distribution is complete, the groom's father gives one spear to the bride's father and then begins eating. This item of tamuk is called the *fegetaw,* literally, 'to ask permission.' The woman's kindred has all eaten before the groom's party has arrived, but the man's side begins to eat only when they see that the fegetaw has been given. While the eating is going on, the buying of the rest of the items tied to the rafters takes place.

The bark containers of food, cooked by the woman's side to be eaten by the groom's party, are considered to be the exchange for the tamuk, so it is important to the pride of the woman's side that they have prepared enough. Every family present with the man must get one container, and, if there are too many of them, they are still taken by the man's kindred and divided among themselves as they wish. A nonrelative of the man who is present at the marriage feast—a kefeduwan, for example, who has attended because of interest in the many tiyawan that usually occur when there is a wedding—cannot join the woman's side in preparing, as that would suggest that he expects to share in the distribution of the tamuk received in the brideprice. Rather, he gives the father of the man one piece of tamuk, thus allying himself for the feast with the groom's side in giving of tamuk. He then, of course, is given a container of food.

By the time all have eaten, the evening is well advanced, and the families in both parties to the marriage have begun to spread their mats, hang their mosquito nets, and put their children down for the night. Couples talk quietly to themselves. A singer may begin to chant one of the many subplots of the *berinarew,* the great Tiruray epic of the adventure of Lagey Lingkuwos, the hero of old who is believed to have led a previous creation of humans to heaven. The kefeduwan gathered begin to discuss the details of past tiyawan,

talking long into the early morning, typically with stories of notoriously difficult situations and particularly elegant decisions.

In the morning, every family cooks for itself, the man's relatives
making use of the rice and chicken bought the day before or provi-
sions that were carried with them. The food for breakfast is not
the responsibility of the girl's kindred.

The tiyawan follows breakfast. Had the entire brideprice been
given at the time of negotiation, as is said to be the right way, there
would not be a tiyawan again at the marriage feast. In fact, there is
almost always an unpaid balance requiring discussion, and it is said
that, should a groom's kindred have given the whole amount prior
to the marriage feast, their standing would be greatly enhanced.
The marriage feast tiyawan therefore usually concerns itself with
three matters: a large amount of the balance is actually given and
accepted, the amount still to be permitted is argued and agreed
upon, and it is arranged precisely which individuals of the man's
side will give and which individuals of the woman's side will receive
each item of brideprice left outstanding after the wedding.

Early in the tiyawan, the kefeduwan of the bride sets forth the
amount of the total brideprice settlement, placing on the floor little
pieces of reed or bamboo as tokens of each item as he had done at
the conclusion of the main negotiation tiyawan when the agreed
brideprice had been summarized. As he does this, he spells out the
portion which, through his side's great pity and kindness, they have
permitted to remain undelivered and reminds the man's kindred of
their pledge to honor the customs and complete every piece prior
to the actual wedding ceremony. The groom's kefeduwan respond
by discussing and offering piece by piece the tamuk they are prepared at this point to deliver. The people on the girl's side, and
particularly her father and kefeduwan, scrutinize each item and
not infrequently express some dissatisfaction with the size of a necklace or the beauty of a kris or the age of a carabao. Should a disagreement of this sort be serious, the kefeduwan present ultimately
give a decision satisfactory to all in their number as to the adequacy
or inadequacy of the item in question, and the tiyawan proceeds to
the next item.

Eventually, in almost all cases, the girl's side will be asked to permit some amount of still undelivered balance. I was not able to elicit from any kefeduwan a rule or even a feeling as to how much should be allowed at that point; their verbal position is invariably that custom requires that no balance remain past the wedding. Nevertheless, in most cases that I observed or heard described, an amount approximating one-fourth of the total was in fact permitted. Where the man's side wished to have much more than this allowed as ungiven balance, the bride's kindred would threaten one of two possible actions. Either they would agree to go on with the wedding only on condition that the couple then return to reside in their place until sufficient tamuk had been delivered, or they would threaten to stop all proceedings forthwith and "kill" that tamuk which had already been given, which is to say, to declare all of the brideprice given thus far to be forfeited. An existing brideprice is regularly spoken of as alive, a forfeited one as dead or killed. This distinction and this way of speaking play a role in the proceedings of hot tiyawan.

When any balance is permitted beyond the wedding ceremony itself, someone in the groom's kindred must accept personal responsibility for each item remaining. He accepts this as an obligation to some particular individual in the woman's kindred who is designated to receive that item, and a date is set by which time the tamuk is to be delivered. Henceforth, the matter is a private one between those two persons. If the required giving does not occur, the two designated individuals deal with the situation—generally through tiyawan, the matter hardly being serious enough to suggest any real threat of revenge killing—but the two parties to the marriage are no longer involved, as such.

Like the brideprice negotiation tiyawan, the marriage feast tiyawan—or any tiyawan, for that matter—is wordy and slow-moving. Hours pass as the various kefeduwan move about verbally from issue to issue, bring in long stories of past tiyawan that they feel are relevant, and seek to reach agreement on the proper settlement. In good tiyawan such as these there is a spirit of accommodation; if the man's side gives so much now and promises to give the rest within such and such a period of time, the girl's side should agree to let the wedding proceed. This spirit is totally absent in hot tiyawan, where the issue is a matter of right and wrong, of fault and the full acceptance of responsibility. Usually the marriage feast tiyawan stretches on past midday, so that once it is finished there is a break for lunch before proceeding to the actual wedding of the couple. Like breakfast, lunch is not the concern of the girl's kindred; each side must prepare for itself.

When all brideprice matters are settled and when all have eaten, the wedding ceremony takes place. A woman from the man's kindred—usually his mother or closest living elder female—goes to the little room where the bride has been staying and, entering, removes the sarong that has been covering her and leads her to the mat where the tiyawan has occurred and where now a pillow has been placed. Three items of tamuk corresponding to these actions have been given during the tiyawan: the *tatas sibey,* 'cut into the room,' the *fuwéh rekeruŋ,* 'remove the sarong,' and the *ʔarak,* 'lead someone.' At the same time an elder male from the man's kindred leads the groom to the mat, where he is placed to the right of the woman. Both face east, so that their lives together will increase in standing and ease just as the sun rises from the east to the zenith. Both sit down side by side on the pillow.

Two *kemeréh,* 'combers,' come forth (a kefeduwan from each party) and stand in front of the couple, the kefeduwan from the man's side in front of the bride and the kefeduwan from the bride's side in front of the groom. As this is happening, the mother of each prepares a betel quid and gives it to her kefeduwan who, in turn, passes it on to her new child-in-law. The couple chew for a few moments, then place the chewed quids upon a bandanna given by someone in the groom's party. The quids will later be wrapped in a banana leaf and hung from the rafters of the house where the wedding occurred.

The two kefeduwan combers then move behind the couple, each again standing behind the person from the other kindred, and begin to comb the hair of the person sitting before them. As each comber combs—the woman's hair first, then the groom's—he gives a speech of advice. The newlywed should be virtuous, faithful, and hardworking and should never cause trouble to the marriage. When the combing and exhortations are finished, the two kefeduwan exchange their combs and give them to the new mothers-in-law. A single plate, containing some rice and a hard-boiled egg cut in two, is then brought to the couple, who, turning to face each other, sit on opposite sides of the plate. Each eats a bit of the rice and a bit of the egg, and the wedding ritual is finished; they are married.

The marriage feast is concluded at this point, and the guests begin immediately to depart. Frequently, however, the kefeduwan will regroup in a rough circle on the floor and begin to settle additional tiyawan that are not related to the wedding, but which are conveniently dealt with at this time since many kefeduwan are present.

The segedot process of marriage-making which has been described may be considered to be the standard, most proper way of uniting a man and a woman (and, in a different sense, of relating their kindred) in marriage. It is not the only way, but before considering briefly the several variants, it is worthwhile to distinguish four features of segedot which, taken together, constitute its propriety. In the first place, both the bride-to-be and the groom-to-be are free to be married to anyone; the kindred of neither has entered into any marriage proceedings on their behalf to anyone else, so that they are not, as Tiruray say, "tied to tamuk." In the second place, the segedot process is morally correct in that it causes no one a bad fedew and necessitates no hot tiyawan. Third, the elders of the couple initiate the formal marriage proceedings, and this is held to be more proper than any situation where the elders are forced to act by the behavior of either or both of the individuals to be wedded. Finally, the arrangements of the marriage are in no way forced by circumstance.

The first of the less proper variant means of marriage-making is called temafus, 'to enclose something,' and differs distinctively from segedot in that the wedding of the couple is accomplished first, by surprise, and only thereafter is the brideprice negotiated and the marriage relationship of the two kindreds properly established. The elders of the man still initiate the proceedings; and temafus, although it creates a sensitive situation, does not in itself cause any bad fedew.

Temafus is not common and is said to occur when a boy's parents wish to have him marry but have had a long series of bad omens when setting forth to initiate the marriage. Waiting until the girl whom they wish to have as their boy's wife is for some reason in their home, the man's mother suddenly places a necklace around the girl's neck and proclaims that they 'enclose' this girl for their son. The act of placing the necklace constitutes the wedding, and the couple is, as of then, married. At the following marriage feast there will be eating and giving of tamuk, but no wedding ceremony, as such.

The tiyawan to negotiate the brideprice, called *sefelasaʔ* and equivalent to the seʔifar tamuk tiyawan in segedot, follows immediately as soon as the girl's parents and her kefeduwan can be summoned. The girl's side opens the tiyawan by stating that, since the man's kindred saw fit to 'enclose' their daughter, they clearly must be well prepared with tamuk; they then state the brideprice. The kefeduwan on both sides will consider that the girl's party has the right to ask a large, though not absurdly large, brideprice under the circumstances and that they rightly have the expectation that the groom's kindred should be ready to give a large part of it at once. Should the man's side not be significantly prepared with tamuk, the girl's side can declare itself to have a bad fedew due to being put to shame by foolish behavior, and the tiyawan changes its character from a good to a hot tiyawan concerned with restitution and fault. In practice this does not occur; the man's parents will not attempt to make a marriage in this way unless they are well prepared. The final business is to set a date for a wedding feast, at which time the girl's relatives will cook and the man's side will give additional tamuk. While all agree that 'enclosing' is not as proper as segedot, still it characteristically leaves both sides with enhanced standing: the girl's side because their daughter was so desired, the man's side for having so much ready tamuk.

A third way of creating a marriage is still less proper than tema-fus, as it involves one of the couple's precipitating the marriage, rather than the elders. Called *temerima*, 'to become a child-in-law,' there are two forms: *malunsud*, where the groom-to-be sets everything in motion, and *lemowot*, where it is the girl who takes the initiative. Neither causes a bad fedew between families, and therefore neither is considered immoral (dufaŋ), however lacking they may be in general respectability. Both forms of temerima are ways of forcing one's parents to negotiate for marriage with a particular individual.

Malunsud begins when a boy simply goes to the house of the girl he wishes to wed, and, when asked his purpose, states publicly to her father that he has come to marry his daughter so-and-so. Immediately the father pretends to be very angry and, grabbing his kris or a bolo, begins to slash the flooring all around where the boy is sitting. While the girl's father is pretending to attack him, the boy sits looking as unafraid and as nonchalant as possible. If he runs away, he is considered to have shamed the daughter of the house and is subject to a hot tiyawan, the interpretation of the scene then being that he had come to do 'foolishness' with the girl and had been driven away. If, on the other hand, he does not run, it signifies that he wants very badly to marry the girl. When the ritual attack is over, the girl's father asks where the boy is from—even if he knows perfectly well—and the suitor replies with the name of his kefeduwan. The father sends for his elders, and the boy spends that night at the house, where he is treated very graciously and fed very nicely by the parents of the girl.

Alternatively, the girl's father may not ritually attack the boy, but rather—if he does not want his daughter to marry him—may send him away. If so, he tells the boy euphemistically that they do not wish their daughter to marry, perhaps claiming that she is sickly, and gives him an item of tamuk 'to cover his shame.'

Otherwise, when the boy's parents and kefeduwan arrive, the brideprice negotiating tiyawan occurs. However disappointed the parents of the boy may be in his clear, public failure to respect their standing, their side would be ashamed not to back him up with the necessary brideprice. What can be given at once is turned over, and a date for the marriage feast is set when additional tamuk is to be given. The couple is wedded at once at a token "feast" in which the girl's parents feed rice and chicken to those people of the man's side who have come for the tiyawan, and the ceremony of combing the couple's hair, giving them betel quid, and letting them eat from a single plate of rice and a common egg is performed. Frequently there is not enough time for proper preparation and collection of

tamuk in advance of the negotiations tiyawan in this type of marriage-making situation, so the kefeduwan on both sides will decide
that the groom cannot take his bride to his own place at once, but
must remain with his in-laws until his kindred has been able to give
a major portion of the brideprice.

Lemowot is the form of temerima in which the girl takes the initiative, usually because she feels that she is growing old and that
no one will ask to marry her. Like malunsud it does not cause a bad
fedew between families and so is morally acceptable, although it is
quite lowering to the standing of the girl. Without telling anyone her
intention, the woman goes alone to the house of a man she wishes
to marry, taking with her a dagger called her *tebeli?* (the name of
a powerful poison, used for suicide). Sitting at the doorstep of the
man's house, she waits for his mother. If anyone else asks her purpose, she says nothing; but when the mother is present the girl says
to her, "I have come to lower myself," and from this the mother
knows that she has come to lemowot. Both sets of parents and their
kefeduwan are called at once; the girl is never sent away for fear
that she will kill herself from shame.

When the elders of both sides are gathered, usually the morning
of the following day, the brideprice tiyawan begins. Invariably at
this tiyawan, the man's side asks the parents of the woman if they
sent their daughter to do this, and her parents say no. This is to allow the elders of the girl to save their pride and standing and to
make the girl carry full responsibility for her actions. The girl's side
then states its brideprice. While they may ask a reasonable amount,
the kefeduwan present will not, under the circumstances, agree to
a brideprice that is excessively high. The man's side states what part
they can give at the time and, whatever it is, the girl's elders must
accept it as sufficient and allow the remainder to be outstanding
balance.

It is said that a girl who goes to lemowot is never just sent away
with a piece of tamuk to cover her shame, because, having so utterly committed her shame publicly, she will certainly commit suicide
if rejected. If the man in question is adamantly opposed to having
her as a wife, his family will seek another man among his relatives

to marry the girl. Should she reject the substitute, she may be sent away; then if she harms herself it cannot be considered the fault of the man's side.

As soon as the brideprice is negotiated, the couple is wedded by being given betel quids to chew. Having so 'lowered' herself, the girl is denied the full wedding ceremonial. There is no feast; her elders are not expected to serve even one chicken, a further signification that they are in no sense responsible for what she did. It is important to note that what the woman did was wrong (she acted bad in her relations within her family), but it was not 'foolish' (she did not cause a bad fedew between families). The husband's side is somewhat proud that the girl wanted him so much; the woman, although lowered, is at least married; and the woman's relatives, though disappointed in what their daughter did, have not been publicly shamed. The girl's side, throughout the proceedings, has taken great care to stress that the shame is not theirs but their daughter's. If all goes well with the marriage, the woman's side will eventually call the man's kindred for a full marriage feast wherein they can properly feed their in-laws and can expect more of the brideprice to be given.

Segedot, temafus, and temerima, although they are of decreasing propriety, are all morally permissible means of establishing a marriage between two persons, neither of whom is bound to a previously existing brideprice. These means are morally permissible because they do not cause a situation where there is a bad fedew between families; they necessitate tiyawan to negotiate and transfer tamuk, but they are all good tiyawan. Later I will discuss a fourth and quite frequently exploited possibility for marriage between uncommitted persons—temaŋar, 'to run away with someone'—as a result of which fedew are indeed made bad and hot tiyawan required if revenge killing is to be avoided. It remains here, however, to discuss a final and important system of morally appropriate marriage-making, in which a deceased spouse is replaced by another individual, so that an existing brideprice relationship between two kindreds may continue undisturbed. One of the common terms used for a brideprice is bilew, 'plates,' taken from the Chinese plate component

of each brideprice, and the Tiruray system of spouse replacement
is called *tundug bilew,* 'chasing the plates' or 'not letting the plates
get away.'

On the seventh day following a person's death, there is a gathering at the individual's house, when certain rituals are performed.
If the deceased was married, one seventh-day event is an important
good tiyawan involving the two kindreds who were party to the
marriage. Their in-law relationship is not altered by the death, as
such, but it is in a sense called into question. It becomes necessary
for them to decide whether and in what way the relationship should
either be perpetuated or discontinued. The fundamental assumption
is that so long as the brideprice given by the man's side is to remain
'alive' and 'away from home' with the woman's side there should be
a correlated living and married man and woman.

If the husband has died, therefore, his widow's kindred, which
is still holding the brideprice that was established at his marriage,
can expect that another man will be *fetindig,* 'made to stand up,' to
replace the deceased as their woman's husband. Should the man's
kindred not put forward an appropriate replacement husband, the
woman's kindred can *fitos,* 'declare as dead,' the brideprice, in which
case it simply ceases to exist. On the other hand, the man's side can
assume the right to 'chase their plates' by putting up such a replacement; and, should the woman's kindred refuse the man they set forward, then they can demand that their tamuk 'come home,' which
is to say that the entire brideprice be returned by the woman's side.
A situation of much the same logic exists when it is the wife who
dies. If the woman's kindred is to keep the brideprice, they must put
forward another woman, and the widower's kindred must accept the
proffered replacement wife if its brideprice is not to be killed.

A replacement must always be of the same structural generation
as the deceased spouse, which is to say, a sibling or a cousin. Prefer-
ence is always accorded to the peer of closest possible degree of collaterality, brothers over first cousins, and so forth. 'Chasing plates'
is viewed as normal and proper, and is the most common cause of
polygynous marriages, as men accept deceased brothers' or cousins'
widows as their own second wives. No woman, however, is ever
required to be a co-wife against her will. Thus, when a husband dies,

the first order of business before a seventh-day tiyawan is often to determine whether the widow is willing to be a co-wife. If so, the man's kindred is free to set forth a brother or cousin of the dead man, even though he is already married, but only if his own first wife is equally willing to have a co-wife.

There can be no replacement spouse unless the tamuk given for the established brideprice is complete. If it was the man who died, the woman's side will not allow another man to stand for him until all outstanding balance is paid in full. Likewise, if a woman dies, her kindred will not replace her with another woman until the brideprice balance is fully liquidated. This must be agreed upon at the seventh-day tiyawan, even though the actual giving of the remainder of the tamuk is postponed until the mourning period is past.

In addition to all outstanding tamuk, the man's side must give an additional amount of Chinese saucers, the quantity customarily being eighty (or eight pesos), although theoretically it is a matter of their choice. Along with the plates, four items of tamuk (by custom, three krises and a spear) are given; these five items are collectively termed the *sila? bala,* literally, a 'bolt of lightning,' and must be given by the man's kindred no matter whether they or the woman's side will be setting forth the replacement spouse.

Moreover, the man's kindred may give a *fegefe?antu?,* 'something to make it new again.' This is an amount of additional tamuk of any size, whether one kris or twenty necklaces. A fegefe?antu? is required if the woman's side has set forward a previously unmarried maiden, but it may be given on the occasion of negotiating any replacement-spouse wedding. It carries the connotation of making it like a new marriage and can, when given voluntarily, symbolize both the husband's intention to really care for his new wife as though she were his first and his intention to act like the real father of any of his new wife's children.

When the mourning period of the widow or widower is over, the widowed person and his or her kindred go to the house of the prospective, agreed-upon replacement spouse, where another good tiyawan is held to confirm the replacement and to accomplish the giving of the sila? bala, any remaining tamuk, and perhaps a fegefe?antu?. If at this tiyawan the man's side is unable to give all that is required, they may offer one item of tamuk and request a postponement. Whether this is granted or not is strictly up to the woman's side and is a demonstration, if permitted, of their being kind. The man's side cannot demand any extension of time beyond the mourning period agreed upon at the seventh-day tiyawan; if they are not prepared to give all outstanding balance, plus sila? bala, the woman's side is considered to have the full right to kill the brideprice. When the brideprice is completed and the sila? bala given—and this is almost invariably the case—they let the woman give her new husband betel quid to chew, and the two are henceforth married.

The procedure described above is that followed in most cases of spouse replacement: the brideprice of the widowed person's marriage is completed and a sila? bala added, and the deceased husband or wife is replaced by a close relative. There are, however, certain important variations.

A widow, and occasionally even a widower, who is quite aged when the spouse dies may decide to remain unmarried and live with their grown children. In that case, it may be decided by the kefeduwan at the seventh-day tiyawan that, instead of putting up a replacement spouse, the kindreds of both the deceased and the widowed persons will set forth an entire replacement couple to be wedded in terms of the existing brideprice. In such cases, too, each person must be a generational peer of the one being replaced, although they may be actually younger people. When both individuals are so replaced, it is considered mandatory that some tamuk be added to the previously existing brideprice, and, of course, all ungiven balance, as well as the sila? bala, must be delivered in the pre-wedding tiyawan.

On rare occasions a married woman in the deceased husband's kindred will 'chase the plates' for her late relative. In such cases, when the man's kindred cannot locate any appropriate man to put forth, one of the women may ask her husband if he is willing to let her chase her brother's or cousin's plates. If he is, and if the widow does not object to being a co-wife, the spouse-replacement procedure will go forward as usual; the man's side will, in a good tiyawan, give any outstanding tamuk along with sila? bala, and the widow will become the agreeing husband's co-wife. Under the circumstances, the relatives of the first wife (the 'plate-chaser') continue to be the "owners" of the brideprice, of course, and not her husband's relatives, although it is the husband and his new wife who are married and who engage in the wedding ceremony of betel chewing.

Although my data include no observed or recorded cases, stories tell of still another possibility open to the man's side if they have no man of the proper generation to set forward in replacement of a deceased husband. The procedure, known as *feŋulambay,* literally, 'to lean against something,' is for the dead man's kindred to ask a nonrelated man (of any generation, but of appropriate age) to stand in for them. He gives the dead man's kindred five items of tamuk and becomes the replacement husband, while they remain the owners of the brideprice. Informants say that, should the brideprice have to "come home" for any reason, the man would also receive back his five pieces of tamuk. As in all the other situations, the context in which the arrangements are negotiated and the tamuk is given is that of a good tiyawan.

In a final pair of variants, a widower does not ask the woman's side for a new wife, although his kindred permits the dead woman's side to retain the brideprice. In both variants the man becomes free to marry anyone he wishes, as he is no longer "tied" to tamuk, but until he does marry the elders of his late wife continue to be in-laws to him and to his elders. When he marries again, they can be expected to give significant help with tamuk for his new brideprice.

The first of these two variant arrangements is referred to as putting the brideprice in the *fantaw,* 'sleeping attic,' which is to say, simply putting it away. This is most typical when a woman dies in childbirth. The brideprice tamuk of that woman is said to have killed her, and the custom is that her husband cannot ask for a replacement wife, for fear that the brideprice will kill again in childbirth. The wife's side at the seventh-day tiyawan gives three pieces of tamuk (generally, though not necessarily, three krises) which are called the *fegefantaw,* 'to put it into the attic,' and the widower is henceforth free to marry anyone so long as a new brideprice is created, at which time his in-laws will give him substantial help. As soon as the new marriage is negotiated, the murderous brideprice

becomes "as though dead," and his previous in-laws cease to have
any relationship with him or his kindred. The husband was never
considered to have had any fault, the tiyawan was not a hot one,
and the offending brideprice, in being placed "in the attic," was not
killed by the woman's kin.

If, for any other reason, the brideprice comes to be thought of
as being bad luck, the kefeduwan may decide that it should be placed
"in the attic":

> Tarbun, an elderly woman of Figel settlement, had been mar-
> ried to three different men, each of whom had died shortly
> after the marriage. The last two had been replacement spouses.
> When Modimfenet, Tarbun's third husband, died, the kefedu-
> wan at the seventh day decided that there should be no more
> replacements as the fourth husband may be also "killed by that
> brideprice." So the woman's side agreed to put it in the attic
> and turned over one kris, one spear, and a large brass betel
> box. The brideprice was put in the attic, and Tarbun remained
> a widow. Although she was free to marry again, she never did
> so.

Still another use of the attic symbol is becoming increasingly
common among Tiruray families that have become sedentary plow
farmers living in the more peasantized areas. Widowers of such
families may not want a replacement wife from the more "back-
ward" people, so they may try to opt out of the spouse-replacement
system completely by asking the woman's side to agree to put the
brideprice in the attic. This is to ask their kindness, of course, because they have a clear right to kill the tamuk if the man's side re-
fuses to accept a woman that they put forward. If the woman's side
agrees, they give three items of tamuk to the man's side, and the
brideprice is in practice simply forgotten by both sides.

The other of the two arrangements whereby the brideprice remains with the dead wife's kindred while the widower is freed from
it is called *segedawan,* 'kindness to each other.'

> Yantuʔ told me this morning about Balaʔud's bringing great
> pride to his relatives through his exercise of kindness. Several
> decades before the Japanese came, Balaʔud married Sambiʔar,

but five years later she died of a swollen thigh. Being already
an important kefeduwan, Bala?ud spoke for himself at the
seventh-day tiyawan. The kefeduwan of Sambi?ar asked him
whether he wished another wife or whether he would prefer
to have his tamuk returned. Bala?ud replied that he did not
wish another woman, that he had been happily married to
Sambi?ar but that she had not borne him any children and had
died very young; perhaps he could not have good luck with
her kindred. They should never mind giving him either a replacement wife or his brideprice. This seldom happens and is
considered an act of great kindness on the part of the husband's kindred and a mark of real affection between the two
sides. Bala?ud had simply surrendered all rights to his tamuk,
not even asking tamuk to put the brideprice in the attic. The
kefeduwan of Sambi?ar declared that this was indeed segedawan, and, as is the custom in such a situation, immediately
gave Bala?ud a handsome kris which is called *tanda?e ro ?eŋa?
ro,* 'they have marked him as their child.' I asked Yantu?
whether Bala?ud had given up the brideprice because he feared
that it was bad luck, and he replied that probably that was part
of it, but that especially it was a great pride to Bala?ud and a
token of his standing as a kefeduwan who is generous with
tamuk. I then asked whether his relatives who had shared in
giving that tamuk would not be displeased at not getting it
back. Just the opposite was the case, according to Yantu?; the
relatives were proud that their side was so kind and generous;
Bala?ud's act had enhanced all of their standing. A few years
later, Bala?ud's next wife, Sewey, also died childless of malaria.
The same offer to Bala?ud was repeated, and he again offered
segedawan. The relatives of Sewey gave him a tanda?e ro ?eŋa?
ro and helped him with tamuk when he remarried, just as the
kindred of Sambi?ar had helped him when he married Sewey.

In good tiyawan, kefeduwan make authoritative decisions about
tamuk. They decide such matters as what amount of brideprice balance should be allowable under a given set of circumstances, what
might be considered reasonable periods of delay for paying the
balance, who should be put forward as a replacement spouse, and
so forth. Although there is ample opportunity to display oratorical
talent and adjudicative subtlety and skill, the atmosphere of the

good tiyawan is happy and relaxed; it is, as the name indicates, good. Perhaps, however, the most important aspect of the good tiyawan is not itself, but its service as a pattern for adjudicating cases of serious dispute where feelings are hot and where fault must be determined and accepted in an atmosphere of considerable tension.

Chapter 5   The Case of ʔAmig

ABOUT a three-hour hike through the mountains from Figel—not very far as Tiruray reckon distances—is a settlement called Keroon Uwa, the place of Moséw, a well-known legal and religious leader. Moséw is a distant relative of Balaʔud, the renowned kefeduwan of Figel, and several of the people from Keroon Uwa are related by various degrees of blood and affinity to people of Figel. Although the two communities are in different neighborhoods, their members do see each other from time to time when hunting the intervening forests or when fishing along the Tran Grande. They occasionally attend each other's religious festivals; they often go to each other's fields at harvest time to share in the work and the yield. Such informal interaction is quite typical of relatively nearby, though not agriculturally associated, settlements. It forms the foundation for many a marriage, as well as for periodic friction and occasional serious trouble.

In July 1966 a large group of the Figel people went along with Balaʔud to Keroon Uwa for an overnight stay. Several minor tiyawan were to take place, none of them serious or threatening danger, and the general spirit of the group suggested a lighthearted excursion. All took their good clothing to wear, especially the unmarried girls, and the hike was at a relaxed pace with singing and much laughing.

At Keroon Uwa, while the women busied themselves with cooking, fetching wood and water, primping, and chatter, the men gathered around the various kefeduwan who had assembled in the house of Moséw. The tiyawan themselves were to begin the following morning, but the men would talk until late into the night about old cases, illustrious leaders, and incisive decisions, about the American who had come to learn their customs, about troublesome Moslem outlaws, about the ways of the homesteaders, and about the pending issues to be adjudicated. During the evening, Balaʔud spoke at length about a situation that concerned ʔAmig, his brother's grandson from Figel neighborhood:

He said that ʔAmig, who was not present, was hot because he understood that someone from Keroon Uwa was still going around saying that he might kill someone. (It seems that Séw, eldest son of Moséw, eloped over a year ago with Binansiya, ʔAmig's wife. Rather than suffer the consequences in the Tiruray system and have to give much tamuk, Moséw—who is a Barrio Captain and thus has one foot in the municipal political structure—attempted a maneuver. He called on the Moslem Chief of Police and some of his cronies, and they frightened Séw and Binansiya into separating and ʔAmig into accepting Binansiya back. They then warned them that if there were further trouble they would fine them three hundred pesos each. A month or so later, some of the Figel and some of the Keroon Uwa men were fishing together. Séw was there and Momiranda, a minor kefeduwan of Keroon Uwa neighborhood. At one point, Momiranda went to Moséw and reported that he had heard ʔAmig say that he was not looking for fish to kill but for a person. There was a tiyawan, but ʔAmig insisted that he never said anything like that and, when Momiranda agreed that he might have heard wrong, the matter was settled without anyone's having fault.) Balaʔud urged all present to consider how dangerous such rumors are for everyone, stressing that ʔAmig was known to be hot-headed and impetuous. He asked that Moséw investigate. Something which is settled once should not come out a second time. The elders should take care, lest there be a killing. Balaʔud said that whoever is saying such

things should be called, that there should be a hot tiyawan, and
that the accuser should be heavily fined.

Throughout his long and earnest speech all listened soberly and
quietly, with only an occasional comment of "that's right" from
Moséw or one of the other kefeduwan.

I learned months later what this episode had really meant. ʔAmig
had not heard any rumors accusing him of murderous intent; he had
grown suspicious that Séw and Binansiya had resumed their affair
and had discussed it with Balaʔud. The old man had taken that opportunity to express the suspicions in an oblique and euphemistic
way and to warn of the potentially dangerous consequences if the
matter were not ended. Balaʔud's point had not been missed by
Moséw, who was also apparently aware of the situation.

When Balaʔud had finished speaking, he sat back and began
to prepare betel. After a moment's silence, Moséw said firmly,
"You are right; it must be stopped; it is very bad." The talk
then turned to other matters.

Unfortunately, Moséw was not able to control his son. In the
middle of October, Binansiya and Séw again ran away together.

ʔAmig and his family lived just across the Tran Grande from
Figel settlement and about two hundred yards upstream in a spot
called Bira. I was away from Figel when the elopement occurred.
When I arrived back a few days later, I found people quite agitated
and concerned. ʔAmig was staying with Balaʔud in the big house.
When he had discovered that Binansiya had gone away with Séw,
leaving her two older children but taking the smallest, he was furious
and went directly to Balaʔud. Balaʔud had talked to him nicely and
persuaded him to eat and to bring the children and his bedding to
the big house until he felt more calm. The kefeduwan had assured
him that he would see to it that he got everything that was coming
to him under the circumstances: his entire brideprice would be returned, and Moséw would have to give an appropriate fine. ʔAmig
ranted a good deal for several days, going around from house to
house, fussing and shouting about his hatred for Binansiya and her

lover and telling of the revenge he and his brother, Soʔ, would surely visit upon their families if his bad fedew were not well cared for
in tiyawan. But he stayed right in the settlement, and, while he spoke
often of revenge, he did not actually do anything precipitate. By
reporting his bad fedew to Balaʔud, by accepting his advice, and by
"trusting his fedew" to him for adjudication, ʔAmig had "respected"
his kefeduwan; he had endorsed his desire for restitution (benal)
to the way of tiyawan rather than taking the way of blood revenge.

As soon as he had calmed ʔAmig down on the day of the trouble,
Balaʔud sent messengers to Moséw, saying that the tiyawan should
be settled without delay. He dispatched two other men to Terefunon, beyond Keroon Uwa, to find Monanah, the father of Binansiya and a minor kefeduwan, calling for him to come to arrange in
tiyawan the return of ʔAmig's brideprice that had been given for his
daughter. To both men, Balaʔud's message spoke sternly of his benal
and his own anger as well as ʔAmig's at the outrage they had suffered, but in calling them to tiyawan he was publishing the fact that
ʔAmig had trusted his fedew to Balaʔud's care and was not after
blood vengeance. Both Moséw and Monanah sent word back to
Balaʔud that they would come to Figel for tiyawan "soon."

ʔAmig returned to Bira after a little more than a week, still hurt
and angry but considerably calmed down. His situation was the
topic of almost continuous discussion among the men of Figel neighborhood and those that stopped for a rest when passing by on the
trail. Late into the night, Balaʔud and the others talked, shouted,
and waved their weapons, alternating stories of how such an affair
can lead to ruthless revenge and has done so in past days, with
comments on the virtues of restraint, the foolishness of Séw and
Binansiya, their own potential ferocity, and the absolute necessity
of getting every single item of tamuk "home" from Monanah, as
well as a substantial fine from Moséw. Most of the talking was done
by ʔAmig's relatives—the shouting by those who were not kefeduwan, the reasoning and reminiscing by those who were. Nonkinsmen
of ʔAmig would mostly listen, nodding in agreement from time to
time, asking questions, and telling occasional tales. Eventually kefeduwan from other places could be expected to join in the tiyawan
themselves as disinterested helpers in the process of fair settlement,

but the affair and the associated hurt and anger being felt at this stage were not theirs.

The morning after he had gone home, ʔAmig was back at Balaʔ-ud's in a rage. He said that one of his chickens was gone and doubtless stolen. If he knew the thief, he shouted, he would surely stab him. A number of people gathered around at the sound of all the shouting, and ʔAmig soon shifted from the loss of his chicken to the loss of his wife.

He (ʔAmig) was very hot and kept saying that if his tiyawan was not soon settled, so that he could see his tamuk come home, he would kill one or perhaps two persons. While he strode about shouting, his relatives gathered around him, but said very little. Mowaniŋ (ʔAmig's first cousin) suggested that the chicken may have just strayed far, looking for food—but ʔAmig growled that he did not care for chickens but for his tamuk. Soon Balaʔud came down to the yard from his house and began to calm ʔAmig, telling him that he must trust him. "When you think I am not interested to fix your fedew," he told him, "that's the time to go killing people. Not now; not so long as you trust me. You watch how I am doing it."

ʔAmig was calmed and persuaded that he should remain at Figel, staying in the big house until the affair could be settled. Balaʔud then sent for Momiliŋ, a Figel neighborhood man married to Binansiya's younger sister, Silah.

Balaʔud is very close to Momiliŋ, who is the son of the old man's second cousin, but, more significantly, the brother of his wife, Legon. He told him privately that he was concerned for the safety of Silah, so long as ʔAmig was so hot. Balaʔud and Momiliŋ then approached ʔAmig and told him that Silah was like a niece to them all at Figel and that he should bear her no ill will for the actions of her foolish sister. ʔAmig was exhorted to respect her husband, his elder kinsman, and also Balaʔud who had her under his care. Then Balaʔud asked Momiliŋ and Silah to care for the feeding of ʔAmig's children while they were staying in Figel settlement—presumably so that he would feel warm toward her for her kindness.

The same evening a large group of Figel neighborhood men gathered in the big house, where there was long and serious discussion of the situation. At various times many of those present spoke, but most of the talking was done by Balaʔud and two minor kefeduwan, Moʔimbek and Mofasiyo.

Balaʔud began with a lengthy lecture advising ʔAmig not to travel around at all, but to stay close to the house, so that he would not receive the blame should any misfortune occur during these days to relatives of Séw or Binansiya. He should not carry any weapons. Above all, he should be patient and just wait, trusting his elders to work this all out for him. The old man stressed that what they want is to get everything settled nicely, to get their tamuk back before anyone is killed. Mofasiyo said that it was not like the old days; by now he would have killed two or three persons himself. Balaʔud recalled that the grandfather of ʔAmig—a kefeduwan—killed another kefeduwan before their tiyawan was settled, stabbing him with a spear from below the house; that, he said, is not the right way. Mofasiyo and Moʔimbek both joined in advising ʔAmig that he should do nothing rash.

Then they all discussed the various coming tiyawan. Most felt that the settlement with Monanah should be first, as he should not be permitted to continue in possession of ʔAmig's brideprice. Balaʔud agreed that it was custom to settle first with Monanah, and then to adjudicate the fault (salaʔ) of Séw. It was decided that another messenger should be sent to Monanah the following day. ʔAmig complained angrily that Monanah was delaying too long, and Balaʔud said that the messenger would give him an ultimatum: either he return their tamuk within two days, or ʔAmig's people would go to Terefunon. Aliman (a field assistant) says this is a threat made primarily to comfort ʔAmig; no one will go to Terefunon to raid. Monanah will come, or send some message. Many of the men present then spoke urging ʔAmig not to be in a hurry.

Balaʔud suggested that if Monanah could not return all the tamuk, they might let him give an 'exchange' (baliwan) to be ʔAmig's wife. Mofasiyo then said that he would go the next

morning to Moséw and try to set a date for that tiyawan; while
there he could urge Moséw to settle quickly with Monanah
and to give Séw's brideprice for Binansiya (so that Monanah
would have tamuk to use in returning ʔAmig's brideprice).

The discussion broke up as men from nearby houses left and
those from other settlements rolled up in their sarongs to sleep. As
I went out, a few were wondering where the two lovers were hiding,
and Balaʔud was admonishing ʔAmig once more to be patient and
to realize that settlements take time.

In the morning it was decided that Mowaniŋ and Moʔimbek
would go with Balaʔud's message to Monanah; they were to tell
Monanah to bring ʔAmig's tamuk to Figel within two days. Some
of the men worried that they might be harmed, as it could be thought
that they were coming for revenge. There were, however, no male
relatives of Monanah in Figel who could have gone more safely, and
Balaʔud pointed out that Monanah had already expressed his willingness to take responsibility in tiyawan and knew that this was the
desire of the Figel group. The two left for Terefunon just before
midmorning accompanied by Mofasiyo, bound for Keroon Uwa
along the way. By early evening Moʔimbek and Mowaniŋ were
back; Monanah would come the following day for the tiyawan.

He did not come. As the day passed, Balaʔud became increasingly concerned and ʔAmig, increasingly angry. The kefeduwan an-
nounced that if Monanah had not arrived by the next morning, he
would send a large group to 'flood' (dunsuk) the place of Monanah.
This was an old term referring to the offended group's going in force
to take revenge, and it caused a bit of excitement among the people
in the big house, although Balaʔud quickly qualified his intention.
The group was merely to get the tamuk or a firm agreement on when
Monanah would come for tiyawan. Seven young to middle-aged
men departed the following day shortly after sunrise. Those who
went were all relatives to ʔAmig, but seemed to have no thought of
revenge. When I asked them if it might occur, everyone stressed
that it was not their purpose. They certainly looked like a war party,
each man with his kris and spear.

Just before dark, six of the seven returned to say that Monanah
was not in Terefunon but was away canvassing help from relatives

in various places, informing them of what had happened, and asking items of tamuk. He was expected back the following day; Mowaniŋ had remained to wait for him. The group reported that when they had passed through Keroon Uwa the people of the settlement had been very frightened, thinking that they were raiding in revenge. The scene was described with great relish:

> Mofaltik (elder brother of Moʔimbek) said that the women had shouted out in fear when they saw his long spear and especially when Mobitam was seen swinging his bolo from side to side—though he was actually just swiping at some small birds along the path. Yantuʔ believed he saw some man running away and speculated (probably fancifully) that it may have been Moséw himself, running in fear for his life. Yantuʔ acted out the fearful flight, amidst much laughter, commenting that Moséw's standing was certainly pushed down.

Many people were gathered in the big house and heard this account of the visit to Terefunon and, in passing, of Keroon Uwa. Earlier, at midday, ʔAmig had gone to Merfangi, a Figel neighborhood settlement a half-hour's hike down river, to the house of his mother, ʔIdeŋ ʔAmig, and his stepfather, Moʔaŋgul. He had said that, since no one was caring for his fedew and since there was still no tiyawan although it was almost two weeks since the elopement, he would fix it himself. His complaint had the effect he doubtless desired, for Moʔaŋgul and ʔIdeŋ ʔAmig hurried to tell Balaʔud. ʔAmig followed, as did other neighbors. The shouts and hot talk of Moʔaŋgul, ʔAmig, and others drew still more to the big house to join the discussion.

A colorful old man, Moʔaŋgul is close to eighty years old, white-haired, foxy, and strong. In 1927 he lost his temper during a tiyawan and speared a man, for which the American authorities sent him to prison for several years. Moʔaŋgul's reputation as a kefeduwan is a curious mixture of admiration and contempt. His skill in oratory is known throughout the Tran area, and all agree that he is a major (*dakel*, 'big') kefeduwan. Most also agree that he is untruthful and self-seeking. Few would trust him with sole care of their fedew or

would, if they were kefeduwan, agree to discuss in a tiyawan with
him if he had no companions to share responsibility for his side.
Balaʔud is his second cousin, and they generally are together in settlements involving Moʔaŋgul. Just after the war Moʔaŋgul, who was
a widower at the time, took the place of a first cousin as husband of
his widow, ʔIdeŋ ʔAmig. Extremely sensitive of his own standing,
he had never gotten along with his hot-heated stepson, ʔAmig—a
long-standing friction that was now painfully out in the open.

The talk in Balaʔud's house was long, very serious, and frequently very loud. I noted down short summations of the points made in
the various drawn-out, verbose, and agitated speeches:

> Moʔaŋgul: This ʔAmig now says he will call his brother Soʔ
> [away harvesting in Timanan] and that they will settle this if
> his elders will not. Does he not have any respect for Balaʔud
> and his father Moʔaŋgul? They cannot talk [i.e., are not kefe-
> duwan; are unable to carry on the complex and roundabout
> debates characteristic of a tiyawan]. Has he no kefeduwan?
> Has he no trustworthy elders?

> ʔIdeŋ ʔAmig (*to her son*): You keep saying this, talking like
> that. If you cannot be stopped from revenge killing, even I,
> your mother, cannot agree to help you.

> Moʔaŋgul (*speaking at length about his troubles with this mar-
> riage from its beginning*): When the brideprice was first ar-
> ranged, there was a dispute about the setuŋoren. It had been
> agreed that I would give one horse for the setuŋoren, but then
> Binansiya's mother had insisted on a large necklace. Later on,
> I worked very diligently to ensure that there were no hard feel-
> ings, going even to the extent of confessing an old, nonexistent
> fault in hospitality to Monanah and giving an extra item of
> tamuk on that basis. Now, after so much help, ʔAmig should
> surely trust me with his fedew.

> ʔIdeŋ ʔAmig (*again to her son*): In addition to that, the child
> is not the owner (géféʔ) of the tamuk; his elders are. If ʔAmig
> goes stabbing anyone, he will not only put his elders in grave
> peril, but will cause them to lose all rights in their tamuk.

BALAʔUD (*joining ʔIdeŋ ʔAmig in warning ʔAmig*): If you cannot be patient, but go to the place of your in-laws and stab someone, you should not expect any help thereafter.

MOʔAŋGUL (*jumping to his feet, interrupting Balaʔud, and pointing at ʔAmig*): It was only this morning, thirteen days after the foolishness, that you came to me! You have no respect. If you do not respect me as your father, I will just forget you as a son and not help at all with any of your tiyawan. Why should I concern myself with ʔAmig if there is no respect and no trust?

ʔAMIG (*shouting right back at his stepfather in a hot voice*): If you will not help me settle my tiyawan, the more I will be hating and will "fix my fedew myself!"

MOʔAŋGUL (*shouting*): I am quite willing to help if I am trusted! (*Then, speaking in a calm voice to all present*) It is my plan to go to Moséw and urge him to help cool ʔAmig off by giving him a peace offering right away.

BALAʔUD (*speaking at length*): Everyone is trying to end the matter as soon as possible; ʔAmig should be patient and should stop threatening to settle it himself by killing.

MOʔAŋGUL (*again interrupting and shouting at ʔAmig*): You can expect no help whatsoever if you go off in disrespect of your elders and act foolishly.

BALAʔUD (*to ʔAmig*): You have already been wronged by Binansiya once before; you should not now be so bothered by what that perpetually foolish woman has done. You should cool down and permit your elders to get their tamuk back and to free you from that Binansiya. Those who are older than you, and have lived longer on this earth, have learned. Once Moʔaŋgul killed, and was sent to the government's prison. I would not want that to happen to you. Moreover, you are young. All you have in this is the woman. The tamuk belongs to your elders, not to you. If you will just trust your elders, then they can see that Monanah returns all the brideprice, or,

The Case of ?Amig

if he cannot, that he gives another woman better and younger than Binansiya. But that can only be if our side is calm, not if we go stabbing.

Mo?AŋGUL (*still clearly irritated*): Without their tamuk, ?Amig would never have had that woman in the first place; now he is always angry and threatening to put everyone in danger. That is not respecting. (*With uncommon frankness toward ?Amig*) No one likes you, and it was difficult to collect tamuk for your brideprice. What do you want—your tamuk or your wife? Tiyawan or blood? If you have no trust or respect for your elders, they will inform Monanah that ?Amig is nothing to them. Whatever you do, it will be alone. Counterrevenge will be your business; the family of Monanah will understand that no one considers ?Amig as a son or kinsman anymore.

?AMIG: I am a bit cooler, and I want the tiyawan.

Before dawn Bala?ud and a few of the other men, including ?Amig, were awake and talking quietly about the many delays in Monanah's coming. As always, the kefeduwan was working to give events an irenic rather than a belligerent interpretation and to understand them in such a way as to calm people and not to incite them, although a different approach to the delays could as easily have resulted in the latter. Bala?ud's main point was that the delay surely meant Monanah was busy visiting his relatives, looking for tamuk to "send home." Mowaniŋ would soon arrive, and Monanah would doubtless be with him, bringing the tamuk. On the other hand, Motoŋ and Mobitam should not proceed with a long-standing plan to attend a wedding along the coast that day; should Monanah not come with Mowaniŋ, Bala?ud might again 'flood' him and force him to come for the tiyawan.

Early in the afternoon, Mowaniŋ arrived from Terefunon accompanied by Mofasiyo, who had gone on from Keroon Uwa and joined him there. Monanah was not along. The messengers reported that Monanah fully acknowledged his daughter's fault and intended either to return the brideprice or to offer another woman. He wanted to see Moséw first, however; he had sent a runner to Keroon Uwa, but Moséw was away overnight to Ugah. The following day, Monanah would go to Keroon Uwa to ask Moséw to accept his responsibility and to be the one to return ʔAmig's brideprice, which tamuk Monanah would then consider to be Séw's brideprice for Binansiya. Otherwise, Monanah planned to threaten to make Séw give a very much higher brideprice than ʔAmig had given. Balaʔud, Moʔaŋgul, Moʔimbek, and ʔAmig discussed this development for a few minutes, and Balaʔud then instructed Mofasiyo to return to Keroon Uwa to witness the tiyawan between Monanah and Moséw. When it was finished, he should bring Monanah directly to Figel to settle their tiyawan. Mofasiyo was to tell Monanah that the Figel people have given him every respect with regard to delays, but now he must come. Otherwise, it might be impossible to prevent violence.

When Mofasiyo had gone, I asked Balaʔud what he thought would probably happen next:

> He said that he was sure Monanah would eventually come and that he was only delayed trying to get tamuk from his relatives, trying to locate a possible exchange woman, or trying to persuade Moséw to settle his brideprice obligations quickly so that tamuk might be available that way. The ideal situation for Monanah would be for Moséw to agree to return ʔAmig's brideprice for Monanah, who would then consider the amount to be Séw's brideprice. If Moséw can gather enough tamuk to help Monanah settle in that way, he can be expected to come with Monanah from Keroon Uwa for the tiyawan in Figel. In that case, Balaʔud and Moséw can tiyawan the peace offering at the same time, and the whole affair will be finished. If Moséw does not help, he probably will not come along—although he will have to make some move very soon to cool the bad fedew of ʔAmig.

Mofasiyo reappeared two days later with the news that Moséw had not yet arrived in Keroon Uwa, and neither had Monanah. While he was still telling of his trip, three women from Keroon Uwa —including the wife of Moséw—arrived bringing a letter which they had received from Ugah to be forwarded to Balaʔud. The note asked Balaʔud to grant Moséw more time, as he was trying to get

tamuk from his relatives in Ugah. The women asked that Balaʔud
not endorse the case to the Maguindanao datu mayor of Upi. Moséw
would surely settle the tiyawan on November 17, in just two weeks.
Although the Figel men had been quite sullen about Mofasiyo's report from Keroon Uwa, the letter made everyone feel much better
toward Moséw. Balaʔud told the women that he and Moʔaŋgul
would be waiting on November 17, and they left for home.

The old man then asked who might go to Terefunon to fetch
Monanah, whether or not he was ready with any tamuk. He should
be told that Balaʔud wanted to settle the tiyawan at once, even if
the brideprice could not be returned on the spot. The tensions had
gone on too long, and he would be willing to accept Monanah's contract to send home the tamuk within a given period of time. At least
there should be the tiyawan, for the sake of ʔAmig's fedew. Mofasiyo
offered to make this trip also and promised to return with Monanah
without fail.

That evening Balaʔud told ʔAmig that his plan was to turn the
case over to the ʔufisina (municipal officials), if Monanah did not
appear the following day.

> He said that he would wait for Monanah to come with Mofa-
> siyo, and, if he did not, he would surely endorse it to the ʔufi-
> sina. Then things would go hard for all who had given them
> such a bad fedew. The mayor would force Monanah and Mo-
> séw to appear by sending policemen after them, he would make
> them return ʔAmig's brideprice, and he would also get a stiff
> fine for himself—300 pesos from each of them. Until they
> could pay that huge amount, the datu would of course jail
> Séw and use Binansiya sexually. The prospect clearly gave
> pleasure to ʔAmig.

In fact, it is extremely doubtful that Balaʔud had any such intention,
beyond keeping ʔAmig manageable. He had already assured Moséw
that he would not report the case to the datu, and it is most unlikely
that, had he done so, the mayor would have concerned himself with
ʔAmig's tamuk (though he would certainly have gotten his fines).
Most significantly, Balaʔud is an ultraconservative traditionalist
with little regard for kefeduwan who reach outside of Tiruray cus-

tom to invoke Maguindanao power for help with their cases. The
idea was, however, useful as a threat as well as a balm for ?Amig.
The datu's bodyguards and henchmen, now officially installed as
the Upi police force, are heavily armed toughs, known for their
rough handling of Tiruray. No official receipt would be issued for
the six hundred pesos, and Séw and Binansiya would not be booked,
though he would be kept in jail and she would be made to work as
a virtual slave in the mayor's household until the amount could be
paid. This would all be a matter of "datu justice" not Philippine
municipal law. The widespread belief among Tiruray that, in such
cases, the datu would make a concubine of the woman is exagger-
ated, but it is believed, and many stories are told of the practice,
which add to the fear of "endorsing it to the datu." Since the American period, when revenge killing was systematically investigated
and punished by lengthy imprisonment, there has been little actual
revenge killing despite perpetual apprehension about it. With the
Moslem datus in political power, the threat that they may enter disputes is now a weighty one. In many ways, it is more credible in
urging for settlement than the traditional, and still deeply felt, fear
of blood revenge.

Monanah arrived with Mofasiyo just before noon, and the tiyawan began at once. This was what Tiruray call a hot tiyawan in
that it concerned a bad, hating fedew, but there was no show of
hostility or anger, only of great earnestness. Monanah came into
the house and without the traditional handclasp sat immediately on
the floor, about five feet to the left of Bala?ud who was in his usual
place. Mo?aŋgul, Mofasiyo, Mo?imbek, and Moliwanan (a kefeduwan from a neighborhood farther up the Tran) sat down at the
same time, forming a rough circle some four meters in diameter. In
the room, sitting just out of the circle, each with his back against a
wall, were seven or eight of the Figel men. Bala?ud's two wives sat
quietly behind the old man, the elder preparing a betel quid for him.
Silah entered the room, and took a place just beside Monanah, her
father.

There were several minutes of silence during which betel was
prepared, but no one spoke. Bala?ud then, speaking quietly,

noted that Monanah had been long in coming. He replied, in the indirect, metaphorical manner of kefeduwan in tiyawan, that he had been held up trying to find the tamuk that should come home during this tiyawan: "I would have come at once, but the way was terribly grassy. I do not know why the way had to be so grassy; my people are slow to cut. I finally decided to disregard the high grass—I knew I must proceed."

The tiyawan was not long or drawn-out. Balaʔud and Moʔaŋgul both made extended speeches recounting the anger of ʔAmig and the patience of the Figel people of ʔAmig's kindred, but the speeches were stern without being hostile. In both, references were made to Monanah's message that he was fully prepared to accept the fault (salaʔ) of his daughter.

[Monanah] listened solemnly, and when Moʔaŋgul finished speaking he spoke out straightforwardly, saying, "I accept my daughter's fault." There was then a moment of silence; Monanah began to tremble and shake. (I learned later that he was suffering from malaria.) He went on, in direct Tiruray, to ask the patience of all kefeduwan present. He intended to ask Moséw to return directly to Balaʔud and Moʔaŋgul an amount of tamuk fully equivalent to the brideprice which ʔAmig's people had given for Binansiya; he would then consider that to be Séw's brideprice for Binansiya. This was the second time that his daughter and Séw had been the cause of danger and shame to him; furthermore, he was ill. If Balaʔud, Moʔaŋgul, and the other kefeduwan present agreed, he would give a *fegefefiyo fedew* (a kind of fine, an item of tamuk here titled 'something to make a fedew good') to settle his relationship with ʔAmig and his kindred. Then, after that, Binansiya and Séw would be Moséw's responsibility. He then placed his kris in the center of the circle of kefeduwan.

Balaʔud replied that rice, well planted, will grow only if granted sun and rain, and handed the kris to Moʔaŋgul.

Here is an illuminating example of kefeduwan rhetoric. Although spoken in the metaphorical manner of tiyawan discourse, Balaʔud's point was clear to all present. He acknowledged, for his part, Mona-

nah's acceptance of his daughter's responsibility; he trusted Monanah's assurance that ?Amig's brideprice would come home from
Moséw; and he was willing to recognize the fegefefiyo fedew as
sufficient under the circumstances to satisfy the desire of ?Amig's
kindred for restitution from that of Binansiya. In using the metaphor
that he did, of benevolent natural elements offering life to well
planted grain, he was inviting his fellow kefeduwan to agree that
Monanah had acted as best he could, had done all in his power to
make things right, under the circumstances.

> There was little more discussion. Most of the kefeduwan pres-
> ent spoke in assent to Bala?ud's judgment, endorsing it as their
> own opinion as well. And when Monanah asked if the tiyawan
> were finished, Mo?aŋgul answered, "finished."

> Monanah was served food, but was still very shaky and ate
> only a few bites before preparing to return to Terefunon. As
> he left, he made the rounds of all present and exchanged with
> them the traditional handclasp.

In the days following the tiyawan with Monanah, life returned
to something like normal in Figel as ?Amig and his people awaited
the coming of Moséw for his tiyawan on November 17. In the eve-
nings the men gathered regularly in the big house to talk, but during
the day they attended to the hunting and fishing tasks appropriate
to the season.

About a week before Moséw was expected, two non-Tiruray arrived in Figel to speak to Bala?ud. They were Maguindanao policemen from Kuya, representatives of the datu mayor and police chief
of Upi—Moséw's superiors in Filipino municipal politics. They informed Bala?ud that they could settle ?Amig's matter in the datu
way if he wished, reminding him that Moséw had called on them to
settle the previous elopement of the couple and that, at that time,
the Chief of Police had promised a heavy fine if it were to happen
again. Bala?ud—intrinsically traditionalist and opposed to kefeduwan's going out of the Tiruray adjudicative system—did not reply
directly, but offered the two Moslem policemen food. As they ate,

the men discussed a rumor that the policemen had carried with them:

> The Moslems told Balaʔud that they understood Moséw was planning to "cheat," that it was rumored that he was claiming that Binansiya was not grabbed from ʔAmig by Séw, but that she had left ʔAmig and was a divorcée. Thus Séw had no fault; he married a divorcée (*gelak*), already separated from ʔAmig. Balaʔud replied that clearly the story could not be true, and that if Moséw attempted to claim such a foolish story, Balaʔud could easily put him to shame publicly. Nevertheless, the old kefeduwan said, should that be his plan, Balaʔud would then endorse the case to the municipal officials.

Balaʔud knew perfectly well that the rumor could not be true. For Binansiya and ʔAmig to have been formally separated there would have had to be a tiyawan between himself or Moʔaŋgul and Monanah, which had not occurred. And, for Binansiya to have married Séw as a divorcée, Moséw and Monanah would have had to meet to negotiate the brideprice. From Monanah's recent tiyawan at Figel, it was clear that no such negotiations had taken place. In accepting the outside intervention *if* Moséw would try to "win" and thus to "cheat"—an eventuality which Balaʔud could discount completely —the kefeduwan had managed to euphemistically dodge the occurrence of such intervention. Assured by Balaʔud that they would be informed if Moséw tried to cheat, the policemen left to return to Kuya.

About one o'clock in the afternoon of the day before the tiyawan with Moséw was to occur, Moséw and a party of close relatives and other companions, including several nonrelated kefeduwan from the Keroon Uwa vicinity, arrived in Figel.

> Moséw's party entered the big house and sat down silently on the floor. Balaʔud was below, advising all the young men not to join in this tiyawan, but to leave it to their elders. Presently he entered and sat down in his usual place. At once, Moséw rose, went to Balaʔud, and gave the traditional handshake with exaggerated elaborateness. He then said, loudly, "Still I may

come to this place?" to which Bala^ʔud answered somberly, "This is the place for our tiyawan." Moséw replied that he was so delayed in coming for tiyawan because he was searching among his relatives for help in the giving of tamuk—thus indicating that he was prepared to accept the fault and settle the issue nicely. Balaʔud, still cool in contrast to Moséw's ingratiating manner, said that the people of Figel have neither appreciated nor found easy the long delay, that they hoped that, at last, it could be settled nicely before anyone was killed. He spoke of Monanah's being very helpful—even offering Moséw his willingness to accept the return of ʔAmig's brideprice as being Séw's new brideprice for Binansiya—of his own patience in not taking his complaint to the municipal office.

Balaʔud, here, in addition to setting forth the outlines of the settlement he anticipated and thus affirming publicly to Moséw that the matter would indeed be settled nicely in tiyawan, was explaining to Moséw that he had not been responsible for the interest taken in the case by the Moslem Chief of Police. If Moséw were to be troubled by any intervention of outside powers, it was his own and not Balaʔud's doing.

Moséw answered that he appreciated the old man's patience, that he was fully prepared to accept his son's fault and to make everything right (fiyo) according to the decision of the attending kefeduwan. Balaʔud, he said, could speak for Monanah. Balaʔud replied that Monanah had made it very clear that he felt Moséw should return ʔAmig's brideprice.

At this point, the conversation became light. Balaʔud, feeling clear with regard to the situation, relaxed markedly and spoke in a jovial manner:

[Balaʔud] told Moséw of Monanah's terrible fits of malaria during their tiyawan. Moséw, chuckling, replied that he doubted that Monanah suffered from mere malaria but guessed that he was also terrified amidst such a multitude of ʔAmig's brave kinsmen. With this, the initial encounter of the two major kefeduwan was finished, and Moséw moved from Balaʔud's side to another part of the room, where he sat among his com-

panions from Keroon Uwa. One of them, Laŋkenan, said to
Bala?ud, "It is all in your hands now what will happen to us—
whether we will be killed or not—for we have come to your
place." Bala?ud answered, "There shall be no killing; tomor-
row, when Mo?aŋgul is here, we shall finish everything nicely
in tiyawan."

The tiyawan began at about seven o'clock the next morning. Mo?-
aŋgul opened with a long and heated account of all the trouble
?Amig had had from his marriage to Binansiya, of the many delays
that had been endured in the settling of the present situation, and
of the extreme patience that ?Amig's kindred had all shown. He
then laid out a series of small pieces of reed, naming them one by
one as the items in ?Amig's brideprice for Binansiya.

When the reeds were all arranged on the mat in the center of
the circle of kefeduwan, Moséw studied them intently without
speaking for several moments, and then said that his son had
the fault (sala?) for ?Amig's bad fedew and that he accepted
that responsibility. He and his companions then set onto the
mat, one by one, eight items of tamuk: three krises, four
necklaces, and a homemade shotgun which was entitled "a
carabao." Each piece was carefully studied by the kefeduwan
in the circle around the mat. Mobinsagan (a minor kefeduwan
of Keroon Uwa neighborhood and a cousin of Moséw) made a
lengthy speech, again reiterating all the facts of the elopement
and the many delays and culminating in an affirmation that
Séw's kindred intended to return every piece of tamuk that
had made up Binansiya's brideprice. He asked, however, for
an extension of time; they could not return all that day. Bala?ud
interrupted Mobinsagan at that point, shouting that further
delays were unacceptable to his fedew. Several of the kefeduwan present then spoke, each using different metaphorical
figures, but, beneath the tiyawan rhetoric, each arguing that,
in such a season of agricultural "hard times," an additional
period to gather the tamuk seemed reasonable. Bala'ud, rather
abruptly, quipped that his stomach was having a "season of
hard times" and that they had all better eat before going on
with the tiyawan. With a laugh, the kefeduwan all dispersed
to eat.

It was then about ten o'clock. Bala?ud's stance at this point is interesting. ?Amig's party had the clear right to restitution (benal), and that had never been challenged. Thus he could refuse to permit any further extension of time without fining Moséw's side substantially. On the other hand, he could grant additional time—a decision clearly favored by the other kefeduwan present—as an act of largess. Possibly, his delay in granting the extra time was in order to hear the opinions of his fellows; equally possibly, it may have been to give dramatic emphasis to his ultimate pity in the face of his benal. As soon as the kefeduwan regrouped, he agreed that three weeks might be given, and, as the other kefeduwan exclaimed quietly, "good (fiyo)," Mobinsagan accepted the three-week period of grace.

> Then he (Bala?ud) asked that Moséw sign a *risibuh*. (The term, from the Spanish *recibo*, 'receipt,' is used of any written document; here the meaning is 'promissory note.' The practice of having such a note is something of a fad and is modeled after known homesteader practice. Whenever a literate person is present at a tiyawan, the kefeduwan are apt to ask him to prepare a risibuh for them. Bala?ud is not here implying that Moséw cannot be trusted.) A promissory note was drawn up (by my Tiruray field assistants, both literate) and signed by Moséw, using his thumbprint. The note, witnessed and thumbprinted by all the other kefeduwan present, listed the tamuk still not returned and specified that it must be given back in three weeks.

Three weeks later, on the specified day, Moséw and a group of companions, including ?Udoy and Wés, two distantly related kefeduwan, arrived in Figel. Bala?ud, Mo?aŋgul, and three visiting kefeduwan were waiting for them, and they began the tiyawan without delay. ?Amig was present to receive the *ta?aŋta?aŋan,* the official 'peace offering' items of tamuk, one from Séw and one from Binansiya:

> Moséw began the tiyawan by asking ?Amig to accept a kris (from Séw) and a brass betel quid box (from Binansiya) as their peace offering. By custom, this is the last thing to be

given in an elopement settlement. Still he asked ʔAmig to accept it right away, to finally put an end to the sense of danger felt by all in Keroon Uwa. The other kefeduwan all nodded and expressed assent; ʔAmig said that his fedew was good, so long as the rest of his brideprice was being returned, and Moʔaŋgul formally accepted the peace offerings on his behalf.

Moséw then gave several pieces of tamuk equivalent to about two-thirds of the remainder, asking that Balaʔud and Moʔaŋgul allow another month for him to locate the rest. Moʔaŋgul protested vigorously in a long speech, arguing that his party had accepted the peace offering in advance of the remaining tamuk out of kindness—to end the danger—and that Moséw should keep his promises without further delay. Balaʔud joined him, in a calmer but firm manner, saying that all tamuk was to be "home" on this day, again rehearsing all the delays and postponements thus far. If Moséw cannot give it then Wés should give it. Otherwise, there should be a new risibuh, signed by Wés, not Moséw.

Here, the call for a *new* contract signed by someone other than Moséw was a clear insinuation of Moséw's untrustworthiness— which Wés, in replying, did not contest. There seemed to be a general consensus that Moséw was delaying unreasonably.

Wés replied to Balaʔud that he had no tamuk now but, given time, would search; he was willing to accept the remaining responsibility (salaʔ). Balaʔud said that this would be all right —but that he wanted a new risibuh! Wés was in the midst of a speech arguing that, since it was impossible to tell how long the search would require, it was difficult to make a new contract, when ʔUdoy interrupted him. ʔUdoy said that Balaʔud's request was proper (fatut); "Can we not accept our salaʔ after so much time? I will sign the risibuh." Wés said that he could give three more items of tamuk at once, and Molalansay (an unrelated kefeduwan, just *tandiŋtandiŋ,* 'helping to decide') offered two pieces.

Wés's attempt to avoid another risibuh was doubtless to spare Moséw the loss of standing it implied; ʔUdoy's rejection of the at-

tempt—and particularly Molalansay's offering to help with tamuk
—constituted a strident rebuke to this line of action. Several kefeduwan expressed themselves with comments of "good" as ʔUdoy and
Molalansay spoke, and, as the latter gave his kris and a spear,
Mobinsagan and Moséw himself ratified the decision by saying,
"It is indeed right (fiyo)." Significantly and irenically, when the
risibuh was drafted, it was Moséw who in fact made the new contract, without any protest from Balaʔud or Moʔaŋgul. Two more
weeks were granted.

Two weeks later, Moséw and Mobinsagan came alone to Figel
and delivered the rest of ʔAmig's brideprice, as well as an item of
tamuk for each of ʔAmig and Binansiya's children. These pieces
are called *bunuʔ* (literally, 'place on one's lap') and are customary
whenever a mother runs away from her family; the bunuʔ signify
that she does care for her children and permit her to visit them in
years to come.

With this last, short, formal tiyawan, the matter was finished.
ʔAmig was now a *gelak*, 'divorcé,' and Binansiya and Séw were man
and wife.

Tiruray moral behavior is aimed at the maintenance, preserva-
tion, and restoration of good fedew; these tiyawan, once the moral
status quo had been disturbed, had the same goals precisely. They
sought to make good, without bloodshed, the hurt and hating fedew
of ʔAmig and his kindred.

The case of ʔAmig has been presented in far greater detail than
I shall attempt with the remaining data. This is partly because my
notebooks contain a richer description of this case than of most,
since I witnessed almost every step in its settlement. But, most importantly, it is in order to give some idea of the comings and goings
of messengers, of the long informal discussions, of the raving and
anger of the one directly hurt, and of the patient concern of the
kefeduwan for soothing and healing—all of which make up the
larger context amidst which formal adjudication takes place in
tiyawan.

Chapter 6   The Hot Tiyawan

EARLIER, under the rubric of morality, I discussed certain key concepts in Tiruray common-sense thinking and their relationship to each other. These may usefully be reviewed briefly at this point, as they stand behind the work of the hot tiyawan.

A person who is hurt (demawet) and made angry (mekerit) by some action of another individual is said to have been caused a bad gall bladder (tété? fedew). As a result, he will have, as Tiruray see it, a perfectly natural sense of intense moral outrage. Whereas, if at all possible, the hurt person ought to try to hold his bad fedew, if it has been caused by a nonrelative he simply may not be able to do so and thus will have an understandable desire for adequate retaliation (benal). The one who did the foolish act (dufaŋ), whether by intention or through culpable imprudence, is at fault and bears the responsibility (sala?) for making the fedew bad. He has thus subjected himself and his kindred to the consequences of the hurt one's seeking, with the help of his kindred, to take vengeance. Since Tiruray understand human nature as likely, when provoked, to burst into a fit of violence and bloodshed, the danger is raised at once that the offended person will seek blood revenge (bono?) and plunge the society into a state of disruption and feuding. The alternative, prescribed by morality as the right (fatut) means of settlement, is to endorse one's case to the kefeduwan, that they may adjudicate it peaceably and properly. A tiyawan called for this purpose will not display the ease and joyfulness of a good tiyawan gathered to negotiate a marriage; it will, in contrast, be angry and tense. It will be *meduf,* a 'hot' tiyawan.

A hot tiyawan, then, occurs when someone with a hurt and bad fedew cannot hold his outrage and seeks a proper settlement rather than blood revenge. This obviously can occur at any time, even in the midst of a good tiyawan, should the discussion grow too heated and become insulting. The important step occurs when the individual with the hurt fedew formally endorses his case to the care of a kefeduwan, accusing someone of 'foolish' behavior and 'trusting his fedew' to that kefeduwan for settlement of his grievance through tiyawan. The kefeduwan will call for the kefeduwan of the foolish one to 'take responsibility for his life,' that is, to represent him in hot tiyawan to settle the dispute.

Although the wrong behavior and the resulting bad fedew are in most instances matters of public knowledge, it may be that the trouble and its settlement both occur privately or, as it is said, *nekoʔ,* 'enclosed in cupped hands.'

Before the war, there was a serious trouble in the place of Modebég, a major kefeduwan of Baka. His son Dumatuʔ, was married to ʔIdeŋ Kew. One day she was discovered by Modebég giving betel quid to a neighbor man, Momasadar—a clear signal that she was his lover. Modebég immediately called for the kefeduwan of ʔIdeŋ Kew and Momasadar, but told them all to keep everything to themselves so that the affair would be nekoʔ. Moʔadas, brother of ʔIdeŋ Kew and an important kefeduwan, came to take responsibility for her life, and the father of Momasadar, a minor kefeduwan, did the same for his son. There was a very hot nekoʔ tiyawan. Modebég asked ʔIdeŋ Kew why she did such a thing, and she admitted that she and Momasadar were lovers. Immediately, Modebég—the aggrieved party—asked Moʔadas and the father of Momasadar to accept their salaʔ and to give a fine of two pieces of tamuk each, which they did. He then told them that they were lucky indeed to be alive, lucky that it was he who saw the foolish couple and not someone who could not have controlled his anger. He asked the two if they wished to return to their spouses and behave themselves; and they said that they did. Modebég then said that they could disperse, that as far as he was concerned, the matter was finished. The father of Momasadar said that he felt his son and his family should move from the place, and the other two kefeduwan agreed. Momasadar moved to his father's place in Kemunsawi. Dumatuʔ and the wife of Momasadar were never told of what had occurred; the tiyawan was kept nekoʔ.

As in this case, the issue of a hot tiyawan is formally stated when a kefeduwan in tiyawan claims a grievance on behalf of the party he represents and accuses some other party or parties of having the fault for his side's bad fedew. The issue, so stated, determines the designations of several roles within the tiyawan. There are, first of all, those in the party who are claiming that they have been in some sense wronged; they therefore are claiming benal, an understandable desire for retaliation; as a group they are known in the tiyawan as the *gebenal,* 'the offended.' In the case just presented, Modebég alone represented the offended party, due to his decision to keep the matter secret. Had ʔIdeŋ Kew's adultery become common knowledge, Dumatuʔ himself would, of course, have had a hating fedew toward the two illicit lovers, and he and his entire kindred would have been the offended side. Furthermore, the relatives of Momasadar's wife would have also had angry fedew and would have been the offended party in a different case against him.

Any party against which the offended side claims a right to retaliation is known, by a derivative term, as the *kebenalan,* 'the offender's side.' In this instance, ʔIdeŋ Kew and her kindred were kebenalan; so, too, were Momasadar and his kindred. These groups, represented by their respective kefeduwan, acknowledged the benal of the offended party in accepting the responsibility for Modebég's bad fedew. It should be noted, however, that, while the entire kindred through their kefeduwan, 'accepts the fault' (salaʔ), they are not all, as a group, held to be 'at fault' (*mensalaʔ*). The mensalaʔ in the case were the two adulterous individuals.

The kefeduwan who are directly involved in a tiyawan, representing either the offended or the offenders, are said to be the owners of the tiyawan. Other kefeduwan who are present and who join in the adjudication of the case, but who are not themselves participating in the dispute under consideration, are known as *tandiŋtandiŋ,* 'helpers,' and a kefeduwan who is present and uninvolved directly and who observes the proceedings without ever joining the discussion is said to be *temanud,* 'watching.'

> The tiyawan (a case involving a broken promise to give tamuk within a certain period of time) dragged on for over six hours. Throughout, Moséw (the major kcfeduwan from nearby Keroon Uwa) sat some distance away, listening intently, though outwardly disinterested. Aliman (a field assistant) told me that Moséw was following the points carefully and would enter if he felt that he could say something genuinely worthwhile. Had he been able to be of clear help in reaching a settlement, the shift from temanud to tandiŋtandiŋ would increase his standing as a big kefeduwan; otherwise he would not bother entering.

Stress must again be placed on the fact that kefeduwan do not contend for their side to "win." They represent their party in the sense that they claim a right to restitution or they stand ready to accept fault, but they all, as kefeduwan, strive together to settle the case properly: to recognize all appropriate rights and to accept all appropriate fault, to the end that cvery fedew will become again good (fiyo), which, to Tiruray, is the state of justice. Because of this characteristic commitment of all kefeduwan present to the achievement of the genuinely just settlement, it is not important how many kefeduwan represent each side. It is generally considered useful for a kefeduwan, particularly a minor one, to have a companion kefeduwan on his side, so that if one should miss a point that is being made in metaphorical speech the other can pick up the discussion. Nevertheless, there may be one or there may be ten; the situation is never that of "one against ten." Similarly, when a hot tiyawan is settled so that trouble is avoided and all fedew are good, the settlement is seen as the joint achievement of all participating kefeduwan and not as a personal triumph or personal defeat for anyone. Moʔadas and the father of Momasadar did their work as kefeduwan with as much credit and respectability as did Modebég; they had not lost and Modebég won. What gives a kefeduwan fame and respect are his achievements in settling tiyawan nicely, his ability shown in again and again participating in settlements that finish the trouble to the satisfaction of all concerned. The skill of a kefeduwan, thus, is understood in terms of his capacity to achieve justice as Tiruray understand that concept, and not in terms of outwitting or otherwise defeating other kefeduwan. As we have seen, to even appear to tend toward such a goal is to invite the severe censure of being called a cheating kefeduwan.

The follower of a kefeduwan is said to trust his fedew to his legal leader. For the offended person, this expression implies his confidence that his kefeduwan, in tiyawan, will see to the appropriate satisfaction of his rightful desire for vengeance; he trusts—and by implication accepts—that his kefeduwan will assure a settlement such that his fedew will again be good. For the offender, his trust of his kefeduwan implies that he will, in accepting the fault, negotiate a fine of appropriate size, one that is neither so large as to be unjustly punitive, nor so small as to be ineffective in repairing the bad fedew caused by his foolishness. In short, all involved trust the various kefeduwan to settle the trouble with complete fairness and, by so doing, to finish the trouble and remove the community from danger of bloody feuding.

I have already discussed at some length various morally acceptable marriage-making situations, each of which could be fixed through good tiyawan. Two general types of situation remain which result in a couple's being married: elopement of two unmarried persons and the circumstances of the case of ʔAmig—elopement of one or two married persons. Both of these cause a bad fedew and are thus immoral modes of marriage; their settlement requires hot tiyawan, if blood revenge is to be avoided. Consideration of these two situations will begin my introduction of the cases of hot tiyawan.

Setaŋar, 'elopement of single persons,' occurs in two forms, both of which are considered to be primarily the fault of the man. In the first, real (*tintu*) setaŋar, the girl is a willing accomplice to the elopement and hence bears a share, although a lesser share, of the

responsibility. In the second, *dagef,* 'abduction,' the girl is carried
away against her will and is free of fault. Both forms are ways of
forcing the elders to make the marriage. 'Real' setaŋar usually comes
because the couple are secret lovers and wish to be married; they
are ashamed to approach their parents directly with their affair; frequently, the girl is already pregnant.

> Shortly after the rice harvest season [1966] Seriŋ, a maiden of
> Dakel Luwan, ran away with Meton, a young man from near-
> by Selaklak. When their elopement became known to their
> parents, messengers were sent to find them and have them
> return, telling them that their marriage would be settled nice-
> ly. The kindreds of the two, with their kefeduwan, met in Dakel
> Luwan for the tiyawan.

The choice of Dakel Luwan, the place of the woman's party in this
case, is dictated by the fact that the tiyawan is, first of all, a hot one.
Only when all fedew are made good will it become a good tiyawan
for the purpose of negotiating the brideprice. Thus the tiyawan occurs at the place of the girl's side, who consider the man's side to
be the offenders, having the basic responsibility for the elopement,
rather than at the place of the man's kefeduwan, as it would in a
simple instance of brideprice negotiation.

> The kefeduwan of Meton readily accepted the fault of his fol-
> lower for having persuaded Seriŋ to do foolishness with him
> and agreed to give the girl's side one kris as *fegefefiyo fedew,*
> 'something to make the fedew good.' They then proceeded to
> negotiate the brideprice.

Couples who have eloped are never forced to separate by the kefeduwan, as it is considered futile, since they will only elope again.
The woman's side is expected to require a usual-sized brideprice,
except that custom in cases of elopement of a maiden precludes
asking the piece of tamuk known as ʔofoʔ seʔifaran. Furthermore,
the woman's side must allow the man's kindred to have as much
unpaid balance (baraʔ) as it needs to have in view of the fact that
the girl contributed to the foolishness and thus removed the leverage over baraʔ usually enjoyed by her kindred.

If the girl does not actually run away with her lover, but becomes pregnant by him, the situation is considered to be the same, and it is treated as a case of tintu setaŋar:

In 1956 Naguyu, a young girl of Baka, found that she was pregnant. She had been lovers for some time with Andal, a young bachelor. Naguyu said nothing to anyone, but after seven months her mother noticed that she was pregnant, and, under considerable pressure from her father, she finally admitted that it was true and that she had been making love with Andal. Her father immediately informed Moʔafut, his cousin and a kefeduwan, of his bad fedew, and Moʔafut sent word to Modebég, Andal's uncle and a major kefeduwan, asking if he would take responsibility for the life of Andal. When they had the tiyawan, Modebég gave a large necklace as fegefefiyo fedew and then agreed to give some of Andal's brideprice at once and the remainder after harvest, at which time there should be a proper marriage feast.

There was not, at the time of the tiyawan nor at the time of the marriage feast, any wedding ritual as such. In cases of elopement the couple is considered to be married on the grounds of their sexual intercourse and their intent to marry, both of which are simply assumed and need not be demonstrated. This contrasts with *menbuwah*, 'adultery,' which I will discuss later; in cases of simple adultery, sexual intercourse may be assumed, but not intent to marry —and therefore the couple is not considered to be married.

The second form of setaŋar, dagef, 'abduction,' is like the first in that both individuals are free to marry, and it too is certainly immoral in that it causes extremely angry fedew on the girl's side. It differs in that the girl is not a willing accomplice, but is simply grabbed by the man. The tiyawan is very hot, and it is the custom regarding a dagef situation that, if it allows the marriage at all, the girl's kindred may insist that the brideprice be given in full without any outstanding balance whatsoever:

I asked him [Balaʔud] to tell me of a case of dagef, and he replied that there had been one quite recently [early in 1965] in Simulawan, a settlement of Keroon Uwa in the mountains northwest of Figel. ꞌUyag, a young unmarried man of Milaya, just up a wooded creek from Simulawan, wanted to marry Lindah, a maiden of Simulawan, but suspected that his parents were interested in some other woman for him.

One day, Lindah went to visit Keroon Uwa, nearby. Usually a young girl will not travel alone, but the path between the two places is grassy rather than forested, and hence easily visible from Lindah's house, except for a small patch of forest along the creek running to Milaya. When Lindah entered that forest, the people in her house heard her scream and shout. They ran to the forest, but could not find Lindah, so followed the creek to Milaya where they found her in the house of ꞌUyag. ꞌUyag had grabbed Lindah and carried her to his home, where he informed his parents that he had abducted her. His father, Mobegon, a minor kefeduwan, scolded his son harshly, saying, "Why did you do this thing? We have no ready tamuk, and now we are put to danger and shame." He then went out to ask help of his nearby relatives. When Molindah, the father of Lindah, arrived at the house of ꞌUyag, he and his relatives were extremely angry about what had happened. The two fathers agreed, however, that they would have the tiyawan the next day in Simulawan; so Molindah returned home, leaving his daughter at Milaya, under the watch of her mother who stayed over with her.[1]

At the tiyawan, Moséw of Keroon Uwa acted as kefeduwan for Lindah and her relatives. Mobegon acted for himself. Mobegon began by accepting his son's fault and asking what his fine should be. Moséw asked him to give one hundred plates and ten pieces of tamuk (a heavy although not unreasonable fine). Mobegon said that he could give it within one week, and this was acceptable to Moséw. Mobegon then asked that it be considered part of the brideprice for the marriage of ꞌUyag and Lindah, asking that Molindah and Moséw pity his side by allowing whatever else should be set as brideprice to remain as ungiven balance for a time.

1. Due to the fact of the setaŋar, Lindah and ꞌUyag are technically man and wife; sexual intercourse is assumed for legal purposes as part of the abduction, even though it had not in this case actually occurred.

At this point, Molindah could accept or reject ꞋUyag as his son-in-law by insisting upon or relaxing the custom that in cases of dagef there should be no outstanding balance. By holding to the custom, he in effect rejected ꞋUyag.

> Molindah replied that he could not consider brideprice so long as his fedew was so hating, that the fegefefiyo fedew fine must be just that and nothing else, and then he would state the brideprice, which, of course, would have to be given in full. On hearing this, Mobegon affirmed that his son had certainly been foolish and that the girl's side had a clear right to the tamuk as fine. He asked if his promise to give the fegefefiyo fedew in a week's time was acceptable, and Moséw said that it was, that the matter was finished. Lindah was no longer married to ꞋUyag, both she and he being considered henceforth as *gelak*, 'divorced persons.' The man's party returned home, and all his elders gave ꞋUyag a severe scolding for putting their lives in such danger, for causing them all great shame, and for costing them much tamuk as well.

The case of ꞋAmig, already described at some length, is an example of the second type of immoral marriage-making, *selamfaꞋ*, 'elopement of a married person.' SelamfaꞋ is extremely common in traditional Tiruray society and is said to have caused a high incidence of blood revenge in the days before American pacification of the Tiruray mountains. Today there is much less actual revenge killing, although fear of it continues to permeate the atmosphere of urgency in which hot tiyawan take place. Anxiety over the danger of blood revenge is nowhere more striking than in the settlement of selamfaꞋ cases.

The various parties involved in a case of selamfaꞋ are designated by terms which derive from the base *lamfaꞋ*, which refers in general to elopement of a married person. (English-speaking Tiruray generally use the inelegant but convenient word "grab.") The two that elope together—Séw and Binansiya in the case of ꞋAmig—are called the *menselamfaꞋ*, which has the literal meaning of 'those who eloped with each other.' Séw himself, the one who 'grabbed' a married person, is the *lemenamfaꞋ*, a term which extends to his whole kindred until the matter is settled. Thus in the tiyawan proceedings which were described, Moséw (Séw's father), Mobinsagan (his father's cousin), and all the rest of Séw's Keroon Uwa close relatives were collectively members of the lemenamfaʔ. Binansiya, the one grabbed, is called the *lenamfaʔ*, and this term too extends to her involved kindred; Monanah, her father and the *kefeduwan* of her party in the tiyawan, was representing the lenamfaʔ side. ʔAmig and his kindred, from which Binansiya was grabbed, are designated the *lenamfaʔan;* Balaʔud and Moʔaŋgul were accordingly the kefeduwan speaking for the lenamfaʔan.

Elopement of a married person throws brideprice relations all out of kilter. As soon as the two have eloped they are considered wedded, and previous conjugal bonds of which they have been a part are terminated. This means that brideprice relationships between the involved families are not in accord with the actual marital situation created by the elopement. To the anger of the relatives of the cuckolded husband, his runaway wife's party still holds their tamuk, even though the elopement of the girl with another man has cut away any right her kindred has to it. Fearing this just anger of the husband's relatives, the girl's side has bad fedew toward the eloper for putting them in such danger. Moreover, the eloping man is now wedded to the woman he grabbed without having negotiated or given any proper brideprice; this multiplies the impropriety of the situation and the anger of the girl's relatives toward the eloping man and his kindred. Finally, the husband has obviously suffered a major blow to his pride and his standing, so that his fedew and those of his relatives are hurt and hating and are seeking some proper retaliation. At least, they want their brideprice back from the girl's side and some personal fine from the offending man and woman.

Settlement of these various grievances, if they are not to result in revenge killing, involves at least three different hot tiyawan.

First of all, there must be a settlement between the cuckolded party and the wife's side, to deal with the brideprice which the former had given to the latter on behalf of the now runaway girl. This was the concern of the tiyawan between Monanah, Binansiya's father, and Balaʔud and Moʔaŋgul representing ʔAmig. The situation is somewhat like a hot version of a spouse-replacement problem

in which the female spouse has died; the woman's party is in possession of a brideprice from the man's side, for which no woman is
presently given. There are, however, certain differences in the customs concerning settlement. Unlike the simple spouse-replacement
circumstances, the wife here did not die but rather eloped with another man—thus there is in selamafaʔ a bad fedew on the part of the
husband's kindred toward the woman's party. Because of this Monanah gave ʔAmig's side a fegefefiyo fedew fine of one kris. Furthermore, while the woman's side may offer to replace the grabbed
woman, the man's side is not required to accept this offer as it
would be if the original spouse had died. In the wake of the elopement, the relationship between the two families is strained, and the
man's side may simply bring it to a close by demanding all tamuk
back. Finally, it may, in fact, ask for the tamuk back, doubled. This
custom-established option is seldom invoked, but it does exist and
it gives the husband's kefeduwan certain additional leverage in
insisting upon prompt and full repayment of the original brideprice.

The second necessary settlement in selamfaʔ cases is between the
families of the couple that eloped. Monanah's side had two grievances toward Moséw. In the first place, Séw's elopement with
Binansiya had placed Binansiya's kindred in grave danger of revenge from ʔAmig and his kinsmen, which gave them a bad fedew
toward Moséw's group. Moreover, Séw now had Binansiya as a wife
without their having negotiated and received a proper brideprice.
Normally, these issues would require settlement in hot tiyawan between the two parties, and it will be recalled that Monanah had
made several efforts to contact and hold tiyawan with Moséw. In
this particular case, however, the tiyawan did not occur. Monanah
had publicized his desire that Moséw return ʔAmig's brideprice, in
which case it would both serve as Séw's new brideprice for Binansiya and make Monanah's fedew good. Moséw did just this and
never engaged in formal tiyawan with Binansiya's people.

Finally, peace must be made between the cuckolded man and the
eloped couple. Their formal acceptance of fault toward the wronged
husband and his formal disavowal of further anger toward them is
accomplished at a small, though technically hot, tiyawan in which
a peace offering of two pieces of tamuk is given and accepted. This

offering, one item of fine from each of the lovers, is called the *taʔaŋtaʔaŋan*, and it is delivered not by the couple themselves but by their kefeduwan. It is accepted by the kefeduwan of the wronged man's kindred and given to the ex-husband. Only after this can the lovers meet the wronged husband face-to-face without danger of violence. Its delivery signifies that the trouble is completely finished, and the atmosphere of danger is gone. The eloped mother may then give a piece of tamuk to each of her abandoned children at any time, establishing that she still cares for them.

It sometimes happens that someone will 'grab' a widow during her year of mourning and before her replacement husband has been chosen. In such a case, she is without husband when she runs away with her lover, but she is nonetheless tied to an existing brideprice. The situation is therefore referred to as selamfaʔ or, more precisely, as *selamfaʔ tamuk*, 'elopement with a brideprice.' There is no wronged husband, but the same kindreds are involved as in ordinary selamfaʔ, and the same settlements are required.

It is not only the making of marriages which necessitate tiyawan— good or hot, depending on the circumstances. Keeping them in repair or, that failing, terminating them with divorce often involves the soothing of bad fedew through hot tiyawan. Some examples follow:

In 1951 Siluʔ was married to ʔOmfoŋ, a thirteen-year-old girl of Buludan. Throughout their first year of marriage, ʔOmfoŋ remained a virgin, refusing to allow Siluʔ to approach her and refusing to cook for him or otherwise help him in his home or field work. (This situation is known as *ʔendaʔ mifat*, 'not caring.') Every few weeks she would run home to her family, and her father would promptly return her to Siluʔ. Finally Siluʔ became angry and said that he did not want a wife who could not care for him. There was a tiyawan at Buludan in which ʔOmfoŋ's side agreed to return his entire brideprice. In addition, ʔOmfoŋ's kefeduwan offered Siluʔ's side—represented by Balaʔud—a large betel box as fegefefiyo fedew. Balaʔud accepted the box, but said that it was a *renuranan tamuk,* 'carrying crate for the returning tamuk,' rather than a fegefefiyo fedew.

The latter is, as we have seen in other cases, the fedew-repairing
fine and implies fault on the part of ʔOmfoŋ toward Siluʔ, a connotation absent from the renuranan tamuk. By renaming the betel box,
Balaʔud signified that in retrospect the tiyawan was to be looked
upon as good rather than as hot and that ʔOmfoŋ's side was without responsibility for a bad fedew, the conclusion presumably being
that the girl was simply young and frivolous. Had ʔOmfoŋ been an
older woman who had stubbornly refused to act as wife despite the
brideprice and marriage, Balaʔud would very likely have accepted
the box as fegefefiyo fedew, signifying that the tiyawan had indeed
been hot and had dealt with hurt and angry feelings.

The wife, in turn, has a right to be treated as a wife by her husband and will be hurt if she is not:

> In the early fifties ʔUguh and Yaŋek became lovers and were
> hastily married. About two years later, Yaŋek ran away from
> her husband and reported that ʔUguh had lost interest in her,
> was not nice to her any more, and would not sleep with her.
> Immediately, her kefeduwan sent word that they were killing
> the tamuk. At the tiyawan, ʔUguh's party asked that the bride-
> price remain alive and that they might replace ʔUguh with Soʔ,
> his younger half brother, as the husband of Yaŋek. The wom-
> an's side agreed, providing that all unpaid balance be given
> first, plus several additional items of tamuk. This was done,
> and Soʔ became Yaŋek's husband. ʔUguh was henceforth
> a gelak, 'divorcé.'

In this case, both sides clearly grant Yaŋek's right to be wedded
to a husband who will act as such. The model for the settlement was
taken from the spouse-replacement procedure: her spouse was replaced by the man's side, all outstanding brideprice was given, plus
an amount equivalent to the five items of tamuk (silaʔ bala) in
ordinary spouse replacement.

Polygynous marriage, while relatively uncommon, exists and of-
fers abundant possibilities for friction between the co-wives. If he
can, the husband settles the difficulties within the privacy of his
household, but otherwise a tiyawan is called for. The following case

involves the rights of the first wife (tafay bawag) to primacy among
the co-wives in the management of household subsistence:

> Tambiyasan had two wives, ?Iden Findinen and ?Iden Mitam.
> One morning, he and ?Iden Mitam went to Barurao market, In
> the afternoon, when they returned home, they found ?Iden
> Findinen—the tafay bawag—very angry at being left behind.
> No food had been prepared for the returning couple. Tambiya-
> san said to her, "Don't be angry; you are both my women, and
> whatever we got at market will be shared equally among you
> two." He told his first wife to calm down and cook, so that
> they all could eat and get to their work. He then went out to
> gather firewood. Before he got very far, Tambiyasan heard
> loud quarreling in the house. He returned and found the two
> women down on the floor wrestling and pulling each other's
> hair. In the struggle, ?Iden Mitam had bitten her co-wife's
> finger so badly it was bleeding profusely. The husband sepa-
> rated the two women and scolded ?Iden Findinen for not heed-
> ing his warning and for causing so much foolishness that day.
> Angrily, he gave her a solid swat on the buttocks with the
> scabbard of his bolo. ?Iden Fidinen then ran away to her parents
> in Daa Fuyut, leaving behind her small baby.

> Tambiyasan sent word to her to return, that he had not had a
> bad fedew to her, but had simply been scolding her for her
> foolish troublemaking. When she refused to return, he sent
> word again that if she did not come back to her family, he
> would call for the return of his tamuk. Again she refused, and
> Tambiyasan informed his nephew, Malag, a major kefeduwan,
> asking that he call a tiyawan and demand that his brideprice
> come home. A few days later, Tambiyasan and Malag went to
> see ?Iden Findinen's uncle, the kefeduwan that had repre-
> sented her family when she was wedded to Tambiyasan.

> At the tiyawan, Tambiyasan related all that had happened,
> leading to his striking his wife; he told of how he had been
> asking her to return to her family and care for him and their
> baby, and he said that if she would not return he wanted his
> tamuk back. The kefeduwan all quickly agreed that Tambiya-
> san had been wrong to slap his wife. Malag, his nephew, asked

Tambiyasan why he should have two wives if he could not treat them properly—the tafay bawag should not only get to go to the market, but should be able to go alone if she wished. She is the first wife. Malag then gave a brass betel box to the kindred of ʔIdeŋ Findiŋen as fegefefiyo fedew and asked whether ʔIdeŋ Findiŋen would be willing to return. She said that she would. Then Malag gave a long exhortation to her, advising her to watch her temper and to control her jealousy of the young co-wife. It is true, he said, that his uncle was at fault for slapping her under the recent circumstances, but she must not vex him with petulance.

Here, as often in the course of Tiruray tiyawan, the issue at hand was first resolved and then moral advice was given. Malag rejected his uncle's right to strike his first wife on the grounds that she had every reason to have a bad fedew at the way her senior status had been disregarded. He thus took the fault for the incident to his own side, did not press for the return of Tambiyasan's brideprice, and gave a fine to the woman's party as fegefefiyo fedew. However, once the legal issue was finished, he had some words to say to the woman about her reactions to the situation!

Tiruray custom requires that a man receive the permission of his first wife before he takes another:

ʔAduʔ was married to Filisa. In 1961 he 'grabbed' Sarimbar without asking the agreement of Filisa, and, as soon as she heard that ʔAduʔ and Sarimbar had eloped, Filisa ran away to her elders. Once the various tiyawan concerned with the elopement were all settled, ʔAduʔ's kefeduwan called for a tiyawan with the kindred of Filisa. At the tiyawan, Filisa said that she still wanted to be ʔAduʔ's wife, and he said that he wanted her to remain as tafay bawag. The kefeduwan therefore instructed ʔAduʔ's side to give a *fedinsel*. They gave Filisa a large necklace as fedinsel, and she returned to ʔAduʔ.

Fedinsel means literally 'to put something next to the wall,' that is, in a safe place. As a fine, it signifies a tamuk item given to a woman to "store" her safely, a type of fegefefiyo fedew given directly to a woman when her shame is involved in certain contexts.

Had Filisa not wanted to return to ?Adu?, her side would surely have been judged to have the right to kill her brideprice. In that case, they would have given the man's side a single item of tamuk, usually a kris or a spear, called a *fitos*. This would signify that the brideprice relationship was terminated and that the brideprice was confiscated, or, as Tiruray say, killed. This occurred in a somewhat similar case:

> Just before Japanese times, Bilaw married Inan by malunsud, taking her as his second wife, because he was already married to Masalin. He had, however, not asked Masalin whether she wished to have a co-wife. When she learned of his action, she immediately ran home to her elders, taking their small child. Her people called for Bilaw's kefeduwan and in a brief, hot tiyawan gave him one spear as fitos, declaring Bilaw's brideprice to be dead. Bilaw's side never disputed their fitos, but several weeks later sent a necklace to show they cared for the child.

A much "hotter" situation—one more likely to lead to bloodshed—is *menbuwah*, a term which literally means 'poured forth' but which is used to refer to one spouse's actually catching the other having sexual intercourse with a lover. In such a case, when adultery is revealed *in flagrante delicto*, it is recognized that the offended spouse will want to kill the two lovers. If this occurs and if both are killed,[2] the one taking revenge is not considered responsible for their deaths; they have the fault for their own deaths. Blood feuding would very likely result, however, so it is here again considered fatut—proper—to endorse the matter to tiyawan for settlement.

> Kison and his wife, ?Entek, were building a house in Megelaway (across the river from Figel settlement and slightly up the mountain). ?Udow was also building a house in Megelaway. One morning, ?Entek, returning from the river where she had gone for water, passed ?Udow gathering wood in the

---

2. It is necessary that *both* lovers be killed. If only one is killed, there is presumption that they were not really caught in the act of sexual intercourse, and the killer is considered to have acted from jealousy. He therefore bears fault for the death.

forest. She and ʔUdow had secretly been lovers for some time.
She whispered for him to follow her, and they went off the trail
a short distance and had sexual intercourse. About that time,
Kison passed by on his way to the river to wash and ran right
into his wife, with ʔUdow standing next to her pulling on his
shorts. He pulled out his bolo, and the two lovers ran off in
different directions. Kison chased ʔUdow, who was running
toward Figel. Moʔekiʔ—an elder of ʔUdow, and also a resident of Megelaway—heard the shouting and ran after Kison.
He overtook him at the river. When he heard Kison's story
and had calmed him down somewhat, Moʔekiʔ told him to accompany him to see Balaʔud, so that the matter could be settled
nicely by tiyawan. Kison agreed. As soon as Balaʔud had heard
what happened, he went with Moliwanag (a kefeduwan, visiting at the time in Figel) to Megelaway to see Buntuŋ, the
father of Kison.

In the tiyawan, which occurred immediately, Balaʔud asked
Buntuŋ, "How many homes do you have?" and Buntuŋ replied, "Only one, here with you," which was to say, the trouble
should be settled peacefully. Balaʔud gave two krises to Buntuŋ, one as fegefefiyo fedew and another as nekoʔ, so that the
foolishness of ʔUdow would not be known by his wife.

ʔUdow's wife never did learn, but the boy's elders were all informed,
and he was extremely ashamed before them of what he had done.
Presumably—although I have no record of it in my notes—some
settlement was also made between Kison's kindred and that of
ʔEntek, who remained married to him.

A final example drawn from those cases where the maintenance
or repair of marriages is at issue involves an accusation of wrong.

[In March 1967] Kufeg went to Basak to buy rice, leaving his
wife, Laydah, at home to plant yams. When he returned late
in the afternoon, he passed by his home, then went to his swidden. Finding Laydah in neither place, he began looking around
and found several footprints by the trail where she had been
planting. He began to feel jealous, thinking that his wife had
a lover. When Kufeg arrived home again he found his wife

there; very angrily he accused her of having a lover. Laydah
was deeply shamed, and ran crying to the big house of Bala?ud,
her "grandfather."

Meanwhile, Kufeg went to Beribud (another settlement about
a quarter of a kilometer away) and told his accusation to Laydah's father, taking him to see the footprints. The father of
Laydah told Kufeg that he doubted that there had been any
foolishness—the footprints were practically on the trail, and
no one would be so silly as to make foolishness right on the
path. Then he went to see Bala?ud. He told the kefeduwan that
his daughter had been put to shame and falsely accused and
that his fedew was very bad to Kufeg. Bala?ud sent a message to
Kufeg that he and his kefeduwan should come to Figel for
tiyawan. The next morning he arrived with Mo?inugal (the
husband of Kufeg's first cousin, and a minor kefeduwan).
Mo?inugal stated that he would "take responsibility for the
life of Kufeg," which is to say he would represent him in tiyawan.

In the tiyawan, Mo?inugal said that he had asked Mo?imbek,
his nephew (and a highly respected minor kefeduwan) to investigate the footprints and that Mo?imbek had reported that
the footprints were no evidence for any sort of foolishness,
being virtually on the path. Therefore, Mo?inugal said that he
would assume Kufeg's accusation as his own and would forthwith declare it to be a foolish accusation; he would put down
one kris and one homemade shotgun as his fine. Bala?ud replied, "Good; finished!" The tiyawan ended with lectures to
all present by Bala?ud and Mo?inugal that quick, unfounded
jealousy can cause everyone trouble. Then all dispersed. The
fine was given to Molaydah, who, in turn, gave the homemade
shotgun to Bala?ud.

Tiyawan may, of course, be utilized to settle an endless variety
of troubles, not only those involving marriages. My records contain
a number of instances of rape or attempted rape, of which the following is representative:

?Ifen (a young married man from a settlement just south of
Awang) was passing by the Dimapatory River, when he hap-

pened to see a woman naked and taking a bath. He waited until she came to the side of the river and then grabbed her and carried her into the bushes. The woman was not embarrassed into submission, but rather shouted loudly for help, so ʔIfen loosened her and tried to persuade her not to tell anyone what he had tried to do. She agreed, just to get away, and immediately went to tell her husband. That very night there was a nekoʔ tiyawan at which ʔIfen's uncle (and his kefeduwan) accepted the fault of his foolish nephew and gave one carabao to the husband of that woman. When the tiyawan was over, the elders of ʔIfen gave him a severe scolding. Later, despite the 'enclosed' and thus hopefully secret tiyawan, the wife of ʔIfen learned what he had done. She ran away to her parents, and, in order to have her return, ʔIfen's elders had to settle another tiyawan and give them one hundred plates plus three items of tamuk. ʔIfen's rash act left him thoroughly ashamed at the trouble he had caused his relatives.

Tiruray are exceedingly careful in how they speak to each other, but there are occasions, generally arising from anger, when an individual is open to charges of being insulting. One such case has already been described, in which the leper Serumfoŋ killed Moŋgoʔ in immediate revenge for being insulted. Insulting, while always extremely risky among Tiruray, need not always result in blood revenge, however:

Kantér (an elderly man whose leg had been withered from birth) kept several pigs near his house in a spot just beside a field which Duriŋ had planted in corn. Several times, Kantér's pigs got loose and entered Duriŋ's cornfield. After warning him three times to keep his pigs tied, Duriŋ could not hold his anger and reported to Bekey (his kefeduwan) that he had a bad fedew to Kantér because of his continual carelessness about the pigs. Bekey called for Kantér, who came to his house with his son-in-law Tayetey. During the tiyawan, Duriŋ grew very hot while telling of his complaint. He accused Kantér of being too lazy to care for his animals properly. Pointing to Kantér's crippled leg, he said, "If you cannot even keep your own body, how much less your pigs; if you were not so lazy, you probably would not have gotten so lame!" This in-

sult infuriated both Kantér and his son-in-law, who shouted
back that Kantér could not be responsible for the way he was
born. There was much shouting and threatening before Bekey
was able to quiet the three men down. Bekey told Duriŋ that
he had a right to be angry about his corn but not to insult anyone. "Look," he said, "these two men came here to settle with
you about your corn; now they are hot and want to kill you;
you are just lucky I was here to protect you from danger."
Bekey told Duriŋ that he must give a fine to Kantér for having
been insulting. Duriŋ, now cooler, agreed and put down five pesos as his fine. Then Bekey returned to the problem of the pigs
and the cornfield. He took the three men to Duriŋ's cornfield
where they paced off the amount of damage that had been done
(an area 40 meters by 40 meters), and then told Kantér that
when his own corn was ready for harvest a portion of equal size
should be given to Duriŋ to be harvested by his wife. That
ended the trouble. Kantér moved his pigs to a different place,
and at harvest Duriŋ's wife was able to gather four sacks of
cobs from Kantér's corn.

Stealing, like insulting, is not a common wrong among traditional
Tiruray, but it does happen on occasion:

In 1964 Mofefeʔ made a swidden in Dakel Luwan, the home
of his father (some four or five kilometers east of Figel). After
harvest, he dried his rice well and stored it in the field hut he
had been occupying. Asking his father to watch his things,
Mofefeʔ and his family returned for a few days' visit to Figel.
One morning while they were gone, the father found that everything in the hut had been stolen: the rice, their chickens,
their cooking pots, even the salt! The father tracked the thief's
footsteps for a way and saw which way they led, but he did not
discover who the thief had been. He then went to Figel to inform and fetch Mofefeʔ.

The two men followed the tracks to their end, coming to a
small house occupied by Mobakey, a religious leader (beliyan)
of Dakel Luwan. They asked Mobakey whether he had seen
anyone carrying rice and other things from Mofefeʔ's house;
he answered that he had not. Meanwhile, they noticed that his

wife was pounding rice of the temaʔiŋ variety (quite large, rounded, reddish grains, easily recognizable). Since only Mofefeʔ had had that kind of seed during the previous planting, they were sure that it was his stolen grain. Mofefeʔ asked Mobakey to return with him to Figel to speak to Balaʔud, but the beliyan refused. With that, Mofefeʔ picked up a handful of the grain and went back to report the whole matter to Balaʔud. The old kefeduwan knew that no one in the general area had had temaʔiŋ seed that year except Mofefeʔ so he sent two men to Dakel Luwan to call Mobakey to tiyawan. When they arrived they found that Mobakey and his family were gone, leaving their house deserted and empty. So, they went back to Figel.

The following morning, Mobakey and six men arrived at Figel, very angry and heavily armed with krises and spears. They told Balaʔud that they had extremely bad fedew because of being falsely accused of stealing. Neither Mobakey nor his six companions were kefeduwan, but Balaʔud said that they should all sit down and hold tiyawan. Speaking in clear language, Balaʔud showed the rice and said that he knew it to be stolen because of its variety and that he knew Mobakey to be committing more foolishness even now. He told Mobakey that it could easily be proven by *tigiʔ* (an autonomic scalding ordeal) and that the beliyan would simply end up ashamed of what he was trying to do. Finally, Mobakey admitted that he had stolen the rice.

The beliyan had attempted to lie and then to end the affair by frightening Balaʔud and the other Figel people with threatened blood vengeance. It is significant, of course, that they were not kefeduwan. Had Mobakey been a kefeduwan, he would have been scorned thereafter as a lemiful, 'cheating,' kefeduwan.

Balaʔud then fined Mobakey 100 plates and ten pieces of tamuk, giving them four days to bring these in, and also all of their arms—several krises, several spears, and a homemade shotgun. The shame of the men was so much the greater when, after arriving with such bluster, they returned home without their weapons. The people of Figel took great pleasure in dis-

cussing that aspect of the outcome. Immediately after this incident, Mobakey transferred his family to Kalamansig, far
away on the coast.

The various cases that have been described are examples of disputes
which are taken into tiyawan when someone reports to his kefeduwan that his fedew has been hurt. In each case, the issue emerges
formally when the kefeduwan of the one who has a bad fedew
claims a desire for restitution on the part of his party and charges
responsibility for it on the part of someone else. As I have stressed
repeatedly, the kefeduwan for the side accused stands ready to accept the fault if it seems accurately to belong to his party; it is not
the Tiruray way for the kefeduwan representing the accused individual to use what forensic skill he has to "win" for his side. Because of this, and because in the great majority of cases the responsibility of the accused is quite clear, very often the central action of
the kefeduwan of the accused is to move quickly to accept the fault
of his party.

However, this is not the only possibility; there inevitably are
cases where fault is not clearly imputable. In such cases, the kefeduwan of the person accused may very well decline to accept the
fault for his side until the issue has been carefully examined and
until he has, with his fellow kefeduwan present, persuaded himself
that the accusation is validly taken. Indeed, in so doing, he can
expect that the kefeduwan representing the accuser will be as eager
to consider all facts and all aspects of the charge—and be as eager
to reject an unsubstantiated charge—as he is himself.

The point is that the possibility of countering charges does not
mean that the Tiruray have adversary procedure. No proper kefeduwan will attempt to confuse the facts or misrepresent them or in
any other way to argue them, however honestly, simply to advance
his party's welfare in the tiyawan. Any kefeduwan who does so—or
who is even suspected repeatedly of doing so—would be branded
by his fellows as 'cheating.' But, on the other hand, all the kefeduwan participating in a tiyawan will surely listen with care and
respect to an earnest argument that the accused is, in fact, not responsible as charged. And, indeed, such a possibility may be raised

by any kefeduwan, whether he be representing the accusing side, the accused side, or neither side as in the case of the tandiŋtandiŋ, the 'merely helping.'

Accusation of fault might be countered in a tiyawan along any of several lines of disputation. One possibility, of course, would be disagreement over what actually happened. In the case where Kufeg returned home and accused his wife, Laydah, of adultery, the response of the accused side—first her father and then, in the tiyawan, her kefeduwan, Bala?ud—was to argue that no adultery had occurred. And, it will be recalled, they were joined in this opinion by Kufeg's kefeduwan, Mo?inugal, who went right on to accept Kufeg's responsibility for making a false accusation.

Quite another possible counter to the accusation of fault involves disagreement not over what has happened, but over whether what happened is to be considered wrong. The background of a quite complex case, all of which need not be described here, illustrates this form of questioning an accusation:

Téng, the daughter of Moliwanag, was wedded to Lalansay, a young man of Tuwol. A year later, she ran away with another man, Dalikan. In settling the tiyawan with Moliwanag, Dalikan gave most of the agreed-upon brideprice, promising an additional two carabao in two months' time. In settling with the kindred of Lalansay, Moliwanag agreed to return the full brideprice that had been given for Téng. Four months later, however, Dalikan had still not given Moliwanag the two carabao, nor had Moliwanag returned all but a very small portion of Lalansay's brideprice. Repeated warnings from Moliwanag to Dalikan did not produce the carabao, so Moliwanag sent Ansun, Téng's brother, to Kinimi (the place of Dalikan) to fetch Téng home, which Ansun did. About five weeks later, Téng went to Tuwol to visit her sister, who lived in that settlement, and, when Lalansay saw her, he decided to keep her there with him as his wife; Téng agreed and stayed in Tuwol with Lalansay. . . . [At the tiyawan] when Dalikan's party accused Lalansay of 'grabbing' Téng, Lalansay's side denied that selamfa? was in any way involved. Since almost none of his brideprice had ever been returned home, Lalansay, they argued, had merely taken back his wife.

Without going into the complexities of how this matter was ultimately settled—it was, in fact, still unsettled when I left the area—it is clear that the argument here is not over what happened. Lalansay had taken Dalikan's wife to be his own spouse. The argument is that his doing so did not constitute an instance of the wrong of which he was accused; he had not 'grabbed' her from Dalikan, but rather had reclaimed her from her father, who still held his tamuk. Similarly, the decision in the following case did not contest what had happened, but rather how what had happened was to be understood:

> Katin, the wife of Andid (a man from near Ranao) had no living brothers or sisters, so when her father was old and widowed she felt obliged to care for him. Andid, however, was not willing for the old man to live with them, nor would he send substantial material assistance. Finally, when he would never heed her pleas to help her father, Katin left her husband and went to stay with her father. Andid did not go with her, but angrily reported to his kefewuwan, Mo'ibon, that his wife had run away from him. Mo'ibon took the complaint to Katin's kefeduwan for tiyawan. When the situation was fully explained, both kefeduwan agreed that Katin had done the proper (fatut) thing in going to stay with her father to help him. The husband should have joined her in the project, either bringing the old man to his place or going with Katin to her father's place. He therefore had the fault for his own bad fedew; the wife was not at fault for their separation. They called on Andid to follow Katin. When he still refused, the two kefeduwan declared his brideprice to be dead and the marriage dissolved.

Again, that Katin had left Andid was not disputed, but what had happened was not considered to have been wrong; Andid, and not his wife, was responsible for his bad fedew.

A third possible line of refutation of fault is taken when the accused side agrees that the wrong has occurred, but denies responsibility for it. This may be argued in several ways: it may be asserted that the act was neither intentional nor imprudent, it may be said that it was provoked and thus justified by the accuser or some third party, or it may be argued that someone else did the wrong.

As I stated earlier, wrong behavior (dufaŋ) involves intention or imprudence. Absence of intent therefore provides an argument that, even though the accused did what he is accused of, he is still without responsibility. Because Tiruray morality demands so strictly that a person act prudently to avoid any chance of hurting someone else's feelings, the defense of no intent is uncommon and tends ultimately to reduce the argument to a question of proper prudence. Nonetheless it is a possibility. As I mentioned, if a farmer's bolo blade snaps off and cuts another person in the normal course of slashing the forest undergrowth, the farmer is not considered at fault for his companion's wound.

A more common denial of culpable responsibility is an argument that the supposed wrong act was provoked and, given the circumstances, therefore not wrong. Tambiyasan, whose first wife was jealous of his second's going with him to market, justified slapping his senior wife on grounds that she deserved it for her foolish quarreling—an understanding of the situation that was not accepted by the kefeduwan. The point is that Tambiyasan did not deny slapping her, nor did he dispute that slapping is ordinarily wrong. His reasoning was that the responsibility for that particular slapping was not his but his wife's. The same reasoning appears in the general custom that a husband may, without fault, kill his wife and her lover if he catches them in the act of adultery; responsibility for their deaths is felt to be clearly borne by the errant lovers, not the wronged husband.

Finally, an accused side may deny responsibility for a wrong act by the simple assertion that someone else did it. This was the tack taken by Mobakey, the religious leader who stole the rice of Mofefe?, when he feigned great anger claiming to be falsely accused. It was an unsuccessful gambit, and Mobakey ended up so thoroughly ashamed before the moral censure of his neighbors that he had to shift his residence to a far place. When, however, the evidence seems to support such a protestation, an individual accused of wrongdoing can expect the support of kefeduwan in his contention that some other person committed the foolishness.

This situation, more than any other, can thoroughly deadlock a hot tiyawan. The kefeduwan that are convinced that an individual is at fault will never agree—for the sake, for instance, of an amicable

or quicker settlement—to concluding the tiyawan without acceptance of that fault. At the same time, those kefeduwan who stand
convinced that the accused is the wrong person will never consent,
so long as this conviction remains, to his side's accepting the responsibility. When a tiyawan reaches such an impasse, it is termed
metigas, 'hard' or 'indestructible,' and there is great apprehension
that the attempt to settle the issue through tiyawan may break down
and yield to violence.

Under such circumstances and when all other efforts to bring
additional witnesses or evidence to bear have been exhausted, Tiruray may turn to a form of autonomic ordeal known as *tigiʔ*:

> He (Moʔinugal, one of the Figel neighborhood kefewduwan
> that has already figured in cases described above) told me of
> observing the administration of tigiʔ. Just before the war, a
> man passed by the settlement of Selungkif (in the mountains
> south of the Upi Valley), and that very day a horse disap-
> peared. They suspected that man and called for him to return
> to Selungkif for tiyawan. The man, who was himself a minor
> kefeduwan, came back and was metigas in denying any knowl-
> edge of the stolen horse. Despite the absence of witnesses, the
> people of the settlement remained certain that he had taken it.
> Finally, it was suggested that the accused man submit to tigiʔ,
> and he agreed. At once, they prepared the pot of rice gruel.

The procedure in tigiʔ is to bring a pot of rice gruel to a rolling boil.
The accused person must plunge his clenched fist into the boiling
gruel and, stretching his arm out, lift the pot above his head, the
steaming liquid pouring down his arm. While there is inevitably
great pain—a fact which certainly must "soften" the stand of many
an actually guilty individual and suggest admission as the more prudent course—the deciding factors are whether the pain can be endured and whether the skin will merely blister or will be removed
altogether. Ability to endure the pain is believed to be a grace given
by the spirit of violence, who lightens the heat of the gruel when the
person is innocent and intensifies it when the individual is lying. En-
durance is established by the accused's being able to lift the pot
above his head; the guilty person would immediately withdraw his

fist the instant it touched the boiling gruel. The skin is watched for
several minutes afterwards; if it merely blisters, the man is innocent, but if the skin peels away, he is guilty.

> Before plunging his fist into the boiling gruel, the accused
> kefeduwan said that if he proved innocent he would expect
> two horses as fegefefiyo fedew for the false accusation. If his
> skin was removed—which he assured them could not happen
> —he would be proved guilty and would give them two horses.
> Many watched the ordeal. The accused person seemed com-
> pletely confident and lifted the pot rapidly over his head. His
> skin blistered but did not peel. When the onlookers saw this,
> they immediately admitted that they were guilty (mensala?)
> of falsely accusing him, and they turned over to him the two
> horses that he deserved.

Tigi?, however, is a drastic and uncommon method for resolving
cases that are deadlocked between an insistence of guilt on one side
and of innocence on the other. More commonly, when it appears
that such a situation has developed, one of the kefeduwan present—
usually one that is neutral, unrelated to either pole of the deadlock
and merely present to help—will declare that he accepts the fault
himself in order to *tafus* it, 'put it into a cage.' The fiction of his
guilt is obvious from his noninvolvement in the issue, and his action
adds to his reputation as a kefeduwan, ready to be generous with
his tamuk to make a fedew good. He thus gives an item of tamuk
to the angry party, the fine being termed both fegefefiyo fedew and
fegetafus, 'that used to put it [the trouble] into a cage.' Where there
has been genuine ambiguity about fault, this generally ends the
situation. The one who could not see justice in his accepting fault
leaves without being found responsible; the one who felt hurt has
tamuk and recognition by the tiyawan of his legitimate desire for
restitution.

The fegetafus arrangement is based on the assumption that the
one protesting his innocence is not lying, for if he were and if the
accusing party knew it perfectly well, the side with the bad fedew
would never accept the fegetafus settlement. The tiyawan would
end without settlement, and a feud would be threatened. It is as-

sumed—and said to be the experience of everyone—that no person would bother to try such a futile play at tiyawan, that since they were inviting revenge anyway they would simply not bother with tiyawan. Thus a tiyawan may be taken, in itself, to represent a genuine effort on all sides to avoid killing and thus to "play it straight."

There are, on rare occasion, circumstances in which it is impossible for anyone to know where fault lies, not because of insufficient evidence but because of inherently ambiguous evidence.

> [In 1914] Basu?'s wife, Dalina, was pregnant, when she became seriously ill with vomiting, hard breathing, and swelling of her stomach. After several days of illness, she died.

It will be remembered that, when a woman dies due to bearing a child, Tiruray consider that her brideprice has killed her, and they do not permit her husband to have a replacement spouse under that brideprice. The husband is free to marry anew; his tamuk is not returned but is "like dead," and three items of tamuk are given the husband's kindred 'to put it [his brideprice] into the attic.'

> At the seventh-day tiyawan of Dalina, the kefeduwan decided that there was no way to know whether the death was due to childbearing or not, and thus no way to know whether the brideprice was the killer or not. Thus it was decided that the case would be dealt with by *sefelawu?en*, 'joining in allowing something to drop': there would be no replacement spouse, but half the brideprice would be returned and half put into the attic. The kindred of Dalina then gave two small krises as one-half of the fegefantaw, 'to put it into the attic.'

Sefelawu?en represents an agreement on all sides to a settlement in which benal and sala? are simply not judged. Instead a mutually agreeable course of action is accepted, and the matter is dropped thereafter. This is seen as an unusual procedure for unusual circumstances, in acceptance of an inherently unresolvable ambiguity about what has taken place.

Sefelawu?en is most emphatically not regarded as a compromise. It is the work of a tiyawan to authoritatively decide fault and set restitution, to the end that all fedew be made good. There is no place whatever in this enterprise for "acceptable compromise":

> Afterwards [a tiyawan had just ended and the people gathered had dispersed], I stayed on and chatted with Balaʔud about his feelings that Maguindanao "datu justice" was so unsatisfying in comparison with Tiruray tiyawan. He said that the trouble with datu settlements is that the datu says something is finished when it really is not. He told me that one time a powerful Moslem along the coast grabbed a Tiruray man's two wives. When the Tiruray leaders went to complain to that Moslem's datu, the datu agreed that his follower should not have taken the Tiruray's wives, so he called for him and ordered him to give back one of the women. The datu then told the Tiruray to be satisfied that the powerful Moslem, who could easily have defeated the Tiruray in a battle, was willing to return even one. He told the Maguindanao to be satisfied with the one woman, lest there be trouble with the "natives." The datu then declared the matter finished. Balaʔud became very agitated in telling the story. The matter was only "finished," he said, because today Tiruray cannot stop the Moslems from their foolishness. How could it be really finished if the Tiruray was still hating? The Tiruray was rightfully outraged (had the benal)—*both* women were his wives, and returning one of them could not make his fedew good. That foolish Moslem was not accepting his fault (salaʔ).

To Tiruray, the issue is salaʔ and benal. Unless these are clearly delineated so that fault can be accepted and righteous anger assuaged through the giving of tamuk, the bad fedew cannot be made good. The issue is justice, as Tiruray understand it, not some socially viable mutual accommodation. The kefeduwan's standing and respect hinge on his ability to conclude settlements in such a way that all fedew are good. The datu's imposition of a compromise based on power realities may satisfy the Maguindanao sense of practical administration, but it deeply offends the Tiruray sense of justice.

In the tiyawan process of seeking to accurately identify salaʔ and to adequately determine and satisfy benal, the original statement of the issue may be greatly redefined. Kufeg initiated a tiyawan by accusing his wife of adultery; the tiyawan ended by fining him for false accusation. Andid reported to his kefeduwan that Katin had run away from him; the settlement killed Andid's tamuk for not having gone with her to join in caring for her father.

In some cases, the settlement redefines the original issue by widening the range of fault:

ʔUtum was married to Ransag in the early 1930s; they had three children, including a daughter ʔEdiʔ. A few years later, ʔUtum died and the following year his cousin, Motabun, was put forth as replacement husband for Ransag. Soon after the war, Mobediʔ (a major kefeduwan from near the coast) 'grabbed' Ransag.

When the tiyawan were settled, it was agreed that ʔEdiʔ would stay with her mother rather than with her abandoned step-father, Motabun, but that when she married her wedding arrangements would all be under the authority of Motabun and his relatives. Not long afterwards, Motabun died, leaving an aged and somewhat senile cousin, Monoŋgon, as the remaining authority over ʔEdiʔ when she married. When ʔEdiʔ did marry, Mobediʔ handled all the arrangements himself without informing Monoŋgon. The old man heard about it eventually and reported to Balaʔud that he had not been respected by Mobediʔ and that he therefore had a bad fedew toward the coastal kefeduwan.

Balaʔud called Mobediʔ for tiyawan. There, Mobediʔ accepted his fault and gave, as fine, one homemade shotgun. Then Balaʔud turned to two companion kefeduwan of Mobediʔ, Momiranda and Mobinsagan. He asked them if they had participated in the making of ʔEdiʔ's marriage. They replied that they had not been present but that they had known of the arrangements being made. Balaʔud then accused them both of contributing to the fault; as kefeduwan, they should have attended and argued against Mobediʔ's action. Both Momiranda and Mobinsagan accepted their complicity, and each gave a kris as his fegefefiyo fedew.

The old man, Monoŋgon, had complained about Mobedi? but not
about the other two kefeduwan; it was only within the tiyawan itself that their part in his bad fedew was proposed and accepted as
valid.

In other cases, sala? may be divided between both parties and a
degree of benal recognized for each. For example, in the following
case of marital dispute, the kefeduwan in tiyawan decided that responsibility was shared:

> Selit, wife of Mosiriŋ, ran away from her husband and told
> her parents that Mosiriŋ beat her continually. So the parents
> of Selit informed their kefeduwan and called a tiyawan to kill
> Mosiriŋ's tamuk.

> At the tiyawan, the various kefeduwan decided that Mosiriŋ
> was at fault for beating his wife repeatedly, which he agreed that
> he did. But, when asked why, Mosiriŋ told the kefeduwan that
> his wife never worked, never prepared food, and never showed
> proper hospitality to guests. When he would ask her nicely
> to do her work, she would have tantrums. So, he beat her.
> When asked, Selit admitted that she had been lazy and prom-
> ised to do better.

> Then, the gathered kefeduwan agreed that, while a husband
> should not beat his wife, he should be able to expect that she
> would do her woman's work. Therefore, they decided that
> Selit bore fault for her beatings as well as her husband. The
> wife's wrong was to aggravate her husband unreasonably;
> Mosiriŋ's wrong was to beat Selit instead of reporting her
> foolish behavior so that his resentment could be fixed nicely
> in tiyawan. Thus the kefeduwan of both sides agreed to accept
> equal shares of responsibility and agreed each to give one kris
> as fine. The two kefeduwan then exchanged their krises.

In all cases of hot tiyawan, once the kefeduwan have determined
the fault to their satisfaction, it is the task of the kefeduwan representing the responsible individual to accept the fault of his follower.
The person at fault is not offended by the decision reached; general-

ly he knows perfectly well that he bears the fault. Even if the issue
is not clear-cut, the one declared to be at fault abides by the decision
of the tiyawan without a bad fedew because he trusts the fairness,
wisdom, and the expertise of the gathered kefeduwan. Just as willingness to accept wrong on the part of his side is the hallmark of a
kefeduwan, manifested in the expression 'he accepts the life of his
follower,' so willingness to accede to his own fault, should his
kefeduwan come to accept it in tiyawan, is explicit in the notion of
'trusting one's fedew to a kefeduwan.'

Having accepted the fault formally, the kefeduwan of the offending side—not the actual offender himself—is responsible for
gathering and giving the tamuk agreed upon as fine. If this fine is
large, some may be given immediately and time may be allowed for
the kefeduwan to canvass the offender's kindred for help in giving
the rest. Always, the kefeduwan of the side bearing fault turns the
fine over in tiyawan to the kefeduwan of the offended side. Then,
after the tiyawan is finished, his kefeduwan turns the fine over to
the individual who has had the bad fedew.

The size of the fine decided upon is based primarily upon the
precedent of past cases. As was mentioned, a good kefeduwan has
a working knowledge of an enormous number of tiyawan, either
witnessed or heard about in the virtually incessant discussions of
old cases that typify kefeduwan conversation. For many recurring
and relatively frequent wrongs, the proper fine has been established
as part of custom; otherwise, the kefeduwan discuss cases felt to
be similar, urging either the same fine or one determined by reasonable interpolation.

In many settlements, the fine is only one piece of tamuk. The size
of the fine should not be grossly inappropriate—the kefeduwan
would never agree to one that seemed to them to be so—but, actually, the amount of the fine is far less important than the fact of the
fine. What counts is that fault has been accepted and reparation
made, honor restored, and, with it, one's good fedew. The movement
of the tamuk as fine—its being given and its being received—sym-
bolizes the accomplishment of this reparation and this restoration.

By custom the wronged individual, having received the fine after
the completion of the tiyawan, will return one item of tamuk from

the fine to his kefeduwan. Since frequently the fine only consists of a single item, he may end up with nothing tangible to accompany the vindication of his bad fedew; but, again, this is not important. How large the fine is and who ultimately receives the tamuk are less significant than its symbolic quality. The fine's occurrence "says" that the matter is finished, that fault has been accepted, that all concerned fedew are good. It expresses, in short, that justice has been accomplished.

It is, thus, the agreement upon and the acceptance of all fault (sala?) and the recognition of appropriate desire for restitution (benal)—the accomplishment of both being symbolized by the movement of tamuk as fine—which bring to an end both the hot tiyawan and the trouble which necessitated it. The tiyawan is finished when all attending kefeduwan have reached common understanding of the sala? involved in the trouble and of the benal involved in its resolution. In doing this, kefeduwan in tiyawan have done what common-sense morality alone cannot do. They have determined authoritatively both the wrong committed and the appropriate response engendered.

Chapter 7   The Tiyawan as Law

THE DEFINITION of "law" or "legal" is a notoriously difficult and elusive problem. As several scholars have pointed out, probably no other central social concept has engendered so much scholarly effort at explanation and definition (Hart 1961:1; Bohannan 1965:33). And a vast, varied, and highly abstract literature has come into existence, devoted to what is surely the most preliminary question of jurisprudence, "What is law?" This question must be discussed briefly here if I am to analyze the foregoing Tiruray data as manifesting a legal system.

In one of the most persuasive and elegant attempts to deal with this question in recent years, H. L. A. Hart argues in *The Concept of Law* that an exhaustive, totally adequate definition of law is probably impossible. Instead, Hart draws attention to the idea of a rule, contending that "the key to the science of jurisprudence" lies in the association of certain distinctive kinds of rules (Hart 1961). Legal systems are designated as such not because they all conform to any minimal set of universal criteria, but because they display what Wittgenstein has termed a family resemblance in the sorts and relationships of their constituent rules (Wittgenstein 1958:17, 18; cf. also Bambrough 1966:186–204).

Hart begins by differentiating between behavior which manifests a social practice and that which manifests the existence of a rule.[1] First, whereas deviations from a group habit or practice need not cause criticism or pressure to conform, divergences from a rule generally are regarded as lapses or faults. Second, where there are rules, most people feel justified in criticizing such lapses; that is to say, rules are generally considered to constitute legitimate standards. Third, social standards—unlike social habits—are carried out consciously; those who follow the standard of behavior maintain a reflective, critical attitude toward it. These differences between a social practice and a social rule find expression in normative terminology: "ought," "must," "right," "wrong." Thus, a social habit like taking one's vacation in the summertime will not call forth general assessments of right or wrong, but a social rule such as not smoking in church will (Hart 1961:54–56).

One very important class of social rules consists of those standards which impose obligations. As Hart stresses, one can only understand the general idea of obligation as part of a social situation which includes the existence of accepted rules. The presence of a rule is the proper context for saying that someone has an obligation, because the purpose of such a statement is precisely to apply a rule to someone by asserting that his case falls under that rule. That is, to say that someone has an obligation is to draw a conclusion in a particular case from a general rule. "Obligation" and "duty" are

---

1. As I shall use the terms here, there is an important distinction between rule and standard. By a rule I mean a normative prescription defining obligatory behavior, whether or not it is formulated or held as an idea by the people whose behavior is constrained by it. Thus, if a people all learn that they ought to face the sun at sunrise, they manifest such a rule in their culture by the practice of facing the sun at sunrise and sensing that it would be wrong not to. They need not be able to state the rule as such. "Rule," therefore, as I use the term, is an external, observer's category. "Standard," in contrast, is an internal participant's category—a normative prescription consciously held as such. I make a similar distinction between practice and custom, utilizing the former for any observable behavioral regularity, whether conscious or not. By a custom, I mean a behavioral regularity believed by the people to exist, whether or not it in fact does. Thus "practice" is an external, observer's category; "custom" an internal, participant's category. It follows that rules and practices are manifested to and exist on the analytic level, whereas standards and customs exist on the empirical level.

an important subclass of normative words which direct attention to a standard and to deviations from it and which point to qualities beyond those which generally distinguish social rules from social practices. Standards which impose obligation are of serious social importance—either necessary to the maintenance of social life or a prized part of it—and therefore call forth insistence on conformity and great social pressure against deviation, as well as possible personal sacrifice on behalf of those who enjoy the benefits (Hart 1961:83–88).

Every society has an array of rules which create obligations upon the members of that society, either by exacting behavior which contributes to the society's welfare or by prohibiting behavior which would be harmful. These Hart calls primary rules of obligation: *A* is to be done, whether one wishes to or not; *B* is not to be done, whether one wishes to or not. The rules of morality are examples of primary rules of obligation. They set forth what people ought or ought not to do, according to the normative common sense of their society.

Hart argues that one could conceive, at least theoretically, of a society in which the only means of social control would be the general attitude that its customs were rules of obligation. Such a mythical society, he says, would live only by a "regime of primary rules of obligation."[2] For such a society to maintain itself, the rules would have to restrict violence, theft, and deception to tolerable limits. Furthermore, most people in the society would have to accept the rules, thereby creating sufficient social pressure to restrain the few who did not (Hart 1961:89).

Even if these two requirements were satisfied, a hypothetical social control system which relied exclusively on primary rules of obligation would display the generic weaknesses which I discussed in chapter 2: the rules, being general, would not apply themselves

2. Hart suggests that such societies have been reported in the ethnographic literature (Hart 1961:89) and cites Malinowski (1926) as describing a near approximation of this state (Hart 1961:244). It may be doubted that *any* society exists which is completely without secondary rules, as they are defined here. Hart's society living by "primary rules alone" should be taken as a mythical one comparable to Hobbes's "state of nature" and introduced for the purpose of setting forth his model of law.

clearly to particular situations. Being unalterable, they could not
be deliberately adapted to changing circumstances or to the particular needs of an individual in a particular situation. Being inefficient to maintain, there would be great difficulty in determining
whether a rule had been violated; and, if it had, punishment would
be left to unorganized self-help (Hart 1961:90–91).

The central idea of Hart's thesis is that what usually mitigates
these inherent difficulties of a system of primary rules is the existence in actual cultures of a related but very different sort of
rules, which he terms secondary rules. These rules serve to introduce, modify, and control primary rules. Whereas primary rules
concern actions that individuals must or must not do, secondary
rules are on a different level, for they concern the primary rules.
Furthermore, these secondary rules are of several kinds. To rem-
edy problems of generality, rules of recognition exist to authoritatively identify whether a primary rule is applicable to a particular
situation. To deal with the unalterability difficulty, rules of change
come into play, empowering the introduction of new primary rules
and the elimination of old ones. Rules of change also include private power-conferring rules, which make possible such voluntarily
created structures of rights and duties as wills, contracts, property
transfer, and marriage. Finally, to cope with the maintenance inefficiency involved in diffuse social pressure, secondary rules of adjudication emerge to allow authoritative determination of what, on
a given occasion, actually happened, to identify the individuals authorized to adjudicate, and to define the procedure that they should
follow. Thus, rules of adjudication define many concepts—judge,
court, jurisdiction, and the like—as well as providing in many systems for centralized official sanctions (Hart 1961:91–96).

The presence of rules of recognition, change, and adjudication
within the social control institutions of a society constitutes in Hart's
analysis "what is indisputably a legal system" (Hart 1961:91).
Here, then, is the basis of the family resemblance between legal
systems: all are complex unions of primary and secondary rules.
The substantive content of any or all rules in one system may be
different from that of the rules in another; or, for example, the rules

of adjudication in one system may be much more complex than those of other legal systems; or a particular type of secondary rule —rules of change, for instance—may be abundant and precise in one system and virtually lacking in another. Still, wherever primary rules of obligation are introduced, identified, modified, or controlled in some sense by secondary rules, there one can see the similarity which characterizes legal systems.

Following Hart's analysis of a legal system as a structure of combined primary rules of obligation and secondary rules, and employing his conceptual scheme of secondary rules of recognition, change, and adjudication, I will consider the Tiruray tiyawan system as a manifestation of law.

Tiruray culture displays, of course, an abundance of primary rules of obligation. These are by no means all publicly formulated by Tiruray as specific standards for behavior. As I have discussed at length, the basic rule that one should never cause anyone a bad fedew serves as a pervasive variable standard which sets situations of various sorts into a context in which moral obligation is clarified. In light of the fedew rule, a Tiruray knows, for example, that he must not violate an individual's personal aversion (keʔikaʔan), for to do so will cause him a bad fedew, and this he is obliged not to do. Furthermore, many general standards for behavior—which are, of course, expressions of the primary rule of respect for people's fedew —are overtly and specifically expressed in custom (ʔadat). In adhering to the customs and in applying the fedew standard to situations not specifically covered by the customs, the Tiruray seeks to behave morally by following what can be analyzed as a program of primary rules of moral obligation.

Similarly, the secondary rules of Tiruray culture are not all formulated in the shape of specified standards. The existence of many such rules is demonstrated otherwise, through their application in actual situations. For example, there is no overtly stated general rule of adjudication that specifies that fines should be levied in terms of tamuk items rather than, say, baskets of rice or hours of agricultural labor. Its existence is shown as particular fines are, again and again, established in the course of actual adjudication. The use of tamuk for fines is simply taken for granted by kefeduwan and their fol-

lowers, and hence an observer of Tiruray tiyawan proceedings may
see analytically that such a rule exists and lies behind the actual
instances of its application without being stated explicitly. Other
secondary rules find overt expression in the customs (ʔadat). It is
ʔadat that sets the procedure for establishing a brideprice, but this
is a different kind of ʔadat, analytically, than the customs which
place moral obligation. One *may* establish a brideprice or not, according to one's needs; he is not obliged to do so. Similarly, custom
permits a kefeduwan to represent his followers in tiyawan. It thereby grants him a particular authority; it does not oblige him to exercise it.

The rule of recognition

IT IS the nature of human societies to depend on culturally established "blueprints" or programs for the organization of their behavior, and a central feature of any culture is its understanding of
"common sense." Tiruray, like all people who live within a particular society and who share a common culture, inhabit a symbolically ordered cosmos, a taken-for-granted Tiruray "world"
which is for them the paramount phenomenal reality. Tiruray common sense provides the natural attitude toward that everyday world,
embracing everyday reality in both its cognitive and normative aspects—what "really is" and what "really ought to be"—and thereby
provides a cultural pattern, a model, for prudent and pragmatic
day-to-day behavior.[3]

Geertz has called attention to an important duality in the meaning of the concept of model:

> The term "model" has, however, two senses—an "of" sense
> and a "for" sense—and though these are but aspects of the
> same basic concept they are very much worth distinguishing
> for analytic purposes. In the first, what is stressed is the manip-
> ulation of symbol structures so as to bring them, more or less
> closely, into parallel with the pre-established non-symbolic
> system, as when we grasp how dams work by developing a
> theory of hydraulics or constructing a flow chart. The theory

3. See chapter 2, notes 2–4.

or chart models physical relationships in such a way—i.e., by
expressing their structure in synoptic form—as to render them
apprehensible: it is a model *of* "reality." In the second, what
is stressed is the manipulation of non-symbolic systems in
terms of the relationships expressed in the symbolic, as when
we construct a dam according to the specifications implied in
an hydraulic theory or the conclusions drawn from a flow chart.
Here, the theory is a model under whose guidance physical relationships are organized: it is a model *for* "reality." For psy-
chological and social systems, and for cultural models that we
would not ordinarily refer to as "theories" . . . the case is in
no way different. (Geertz 1966:7)

Ordinary, day-to-day behavior is, in these terms, based upon the
"model for" aspect of the cultural patterns presented by the common-sense model. As I have pointed out, Tiruray morality in general consists of the normative implications of Tiruray common sense.
Because common sense "knows" (cognitively) that nonrelatives
are likely, if hurt, to respond with violence, it "knows" (normative-
ly) that one ought to respect carefully the sensitivities of a neighbor.
And, in general, Tiruray common sense directs role behavior and
interpersonal attitudes which are respectful of the sensitivities of
others; it is a general model for respectful, moral behavior.

By application of the basic moral norm of Tiruray common sense
—the fedew rule—an individual particularizes as best he can the
general obligations of morality as they apply to the specifics of his
precise situation at any given time. The general proscription against
disrespect is thus focused, and particular actions are revealed as
respectful or not with regard to a particular set of existential circumstances.

Application of the fedew rule to a specific situation, then, permits
the general model of common sense to be sharpened into a model
for an individual's right behavior in the precise context of his immediate situation, taking into account all that he knows of the per-
sonalities and the circumstances involved. In this way, behavior can
be undertaken which would not be characterized as simply appropriate or merely effective (ʔarus), but as specifically proper (fatut)
—not only as recognizably Tiruray behavior, but as intentionally

good (fiyo). Similarly, this introduction of the fedew rule into the sizing-up of a particular situation exposes other possible behavior, although it may be equally Tiruray and perhaps just as effective, as being not fiyo but bad (tété?) or immoral (dufaŋ).

In tiyawan when the kefeduwan consider someone's past actions, they perform a parallel application of the common-sense model to that behavior in order to determine whether it was reasonable. More especially, by including reference to the fedew rule as they feel it applies to the situation, they compare a specifically normative model to the actual behavior in order to determine whether it was morally proper. On precisely this inquiry rests their determination of clupability: whether the individual involved has responsibility (sala?) for a bad fedew.

The difference is that, whereas the individual setting out to behave properly applies his notions of normative common sense as a *model for* his actions, kefeduwan retrospectively apply their normative blueprint as a *model of* what should have taken place and thereby make an ex post facto judgment upon what did take place.

Empirically, when kefeduwan in tiyawan determine that such and such a person is at fault for the bad fedew of the offended person— or, put differently, that his action toward the wronged individual was 'foolish' (dufaŋ)—they are making an inference concerning that action in terms of the overarching imperative of the Tiruray fedew rule: that no one should ever cause another person a bad fedew. Analytically, they have decided that, in the light of the fedew rule, the behavior under scrutiny is an instance of the violation of an applicable standard of behavior. It is in precisely this way that kefeduwan in tiyawan authoritatively identify—or recognize—a rule as having been applicable and as having been broken.

The fedew rule thus plays two roles in Tiruray moral-legal culture. For the individual endeavoring to live morally it serves—as part of his model for behavior—as a basic, underlying variable standard in terms of which the individual can clarify his moral obligations in specific situations. Analytically, it is in this setting a supreme primary rule of obligation, a basic moral norm by which the Tiruray identifies the operational norms applicable to him in a given set of circumstances.

For the kefeduwan sitting in judgment upon whether some past behavior was wrong, the fedew rule serves—as part of his model of the behavior that should have occurred—to identify the derivative moral obligations which under the circumstances should have obtained. Analytically, in this retrospective usage the fedew rule serves the kefeduwan as a secondary rule of recognition.

The rule of recognition, like any other rule which is generally accepted, may remain unstated. If a kefeduwan says in the context of a tiyawan that eloping with a man's wife is wrong because it makes the man's fedew bad, he is asserting the validity of an implicit rule against elopement on the basis of an explicit rule of recognition— the fedew rule. From within the culture, merely to assert that an action is wrong or that the one who did it is at fault is to do the same thing, except that the rule of recognition has not been overtly stated. In Tiruray discourse, common acceptance of the fedew rule as identifying an action as wrong may be simply assumed.

The decisions of kefeduwan are, as has been noted, not only publicly made, but are the subject of a great deal of public conversation. The results of tiyawan are common topics of general discussion, and kefeduwan themselves seem never to tire of speaking with each other and with their followers about the origins, course, and outcome of recent or long past tiyawan that they have heard about or participated in.

Previous settlements thus become for the kefeduwan who discuss them a form of precedent, presenting concrete instances of actual behavior as they have been previously interpreted in terms of model behavior. Similarly, of course, each new decision creates new precedent. Kefeduwan about to discuss a case where someone has interfered with another person's bantak, 'plans,' for instance, may be faced with deciding whether the bantak was well enough publicized to reasonably command the respect of other persons and whether it is, itself, reasonable enough to lay a claim upon forbearance. While it is clearly true that similar cases previously decided will not correspond in every detail to the case at hand, it is also true that, in seeing how the bounds of reason were heretofore interpreted in concrete application of the fedew rule, kefeduwan are able to clarify and sharpen their model of what should be considered reasonable. Their decision in the pending case will then serve as a further clarification which may be drawn upon in the future. Tiruray have no formal apparatus for the recording or classification of precedent, but the memory for detail about past tiyawan which characterizes any effective kefeduwan and the propensity of all kefeduwan to rehearse those details in countless conversations out of tiyawan and at key points within them provide a storehouse of precedent which, although informal, is nonetheless effective.

Moreover, because of the public nature both of tiyawan themselves and of kefeduwan discussion about them, there is an important feedback between legal decisions and popular moral notions. It would be an error to see Tiruray law (or any other legal system) as functioning as a means of social control only through the formal settlement of litigation. Of equal or even greater importance is the function of the legal institutions in controlling and guiding people in day-to-day living. Most Tiruray, most of the time, are not involved in tiyawan. They behave, in general, in accordance with their internalized sense of what is right as it is institutionalized into their society's model for moral action. Acting intuitively in most cases, they do not need to work out laboriously how the fedew rule is to apply each and every time. Similarly, kefeduwan most of the time intuitively know what should or should not have been done in a situation they are considering in tiyawan. But, however subconscious or effortless the process may seem, intuitive behavior is learned, culturally modeled behavior. It is a role of past decisions, as witnessed or as learned from oral tradition, to "instruct the intuitions" of both kefeduwan and ordinary individuals. They fill in and sharpen the legal authorities' model *of* what proper behavior should be, and they feed into the people's model *for* achieving proper behavior. As precedent, they aid the kefeduwan to do his work in tiyawan, but they also help the Tiruray individual to stay out of tiyawan.

Whether intuitively or by careful conscious consideration, Tiruray ultimately do arrive at an understanding of the moral obligations implicit in a given situation by their understanding of what custom (ʔadat) is and of what respect (ʔadat) is in that situation. All wrongs—stealing, despising, wife-grabbing—are ultimately wrong because they cause someone a bad fedew, and *anything* can be wrong if it intentionally or through culpable imprudence leads to that end.

Used retrospectively in tiyawan, the fedew rule is the ultimate standard by which any action is judged by kefeduwan to be wrong, to have violated a valid moral obligation. Here we see the union of two analytically quite different kinds of rule. When a person's actions are authoritatively assessed as either right or wrong by kefeduwan in tiyawan, reference is being made implicitly or explicitly to primary rules of obligation. And, since the primary rules are in tiyawan thereby identified as having been or not having been applicable or valid for the situation under consideration, reference is being made implicitly or explicitly to a secondary rule of recognition. The action is judged as to whether it did or did not cause a bad fedew. This is the Tiruray rule of recognition.

Earlier, I suggested that the Tiruray tiyawan system could be seen as an extended case study in support of the general proposition that law may be understood as a structural response to the cultural strain engendered by three practical insufficiencies in morality: the generality, the unalterability, and the maintenance inefficiency of moral rules.

The first difficulty which law remedies is the generality of moral obligation. The primary rules of obligation which are manifest in the operation of a moral system are not specific to certain individuals in certain situations. They are general. They refer to classes of acts, classes of persons, and classes of situations. Their application in any concrete case demands that the situation be identified as a particular instance of the general class subsumed under the rule in question. While many, perhaps most, situations may be quite unambiguous, others will be puzzling and vague; these last, as much as the first, must be classified as being or not being constitutive of moral obligations.

The Tiruray individual who attempts to behave morally tries to clarify problematic situations by applying the fedew rule to them as a variable moral standard, as a basic primary rule. His ultimate decision is still his personal estimate of the situation, however; it is his own evaluation of what the moral obligations are and of what the reasonable demands upon respect are. Others may very well size up the situation differently and feel that his behavior has not been right. The problem here is not in the general rules, which may be perfectly clear, but in the personal decisions as to the rules' applicability to the given, existential circumstances.

In contrast, kefeduwan in tiyawan apply the fedew rule as a secondary rule of recognition and thereby determine—officially and authoritatively—whether a given action was wrong. Thus, kefeduwan working together to settle a case are enabled to solve the problem of the generality of moral rules for that case. Their decision is an affirmation that certain rules were or were not relevant rules of obligation and an unambiguous statement that the action was or was not an instance of the general class of actions covered by those rules.

Just as the substantive content of the primary rules of obligation may be vastly different from one legal system to another, so the institutional forms elaborated as a result of any particular rule of recognition may vary greatly in different cultures. A striking case is the absence in the Tiruray system of any institutionalized body of laws. Legal recognition of validity is given to particular moral rules for the purpose of particular cases, but the moral rules remain only as moral rules. They are not selected out and codified into a *corpus juris*. As I have pointed out, the Tiruray operate without any official legislature, and this has several significant consequences. While it means that there is very little capacity to adapt the primary rules of obligation to changing needs in changing times, it also means that primary rules of obligation are not institutionalized, as in many cultures, into two separate systems—one moral and the other legal. Where there is such a double institutionalization, the moral code and the legal code are launched on separate institutional histories and the way is open for each to develop somewhat differently from the other in accordance with its own internal logic.[4] It is clear that in the United States, for example, rulings of the Supreme Court that

4. The term "double institutionalization" is Bohannan's (1965:34 ff.). From the point of view accepted here, it is not inevitable that legal norms be doubly institutionalized, and thus it is also not inevitable that "law is always out of phase with society" (Bohannan 1965:37).

are made according to the logic of the law, as that body understands it, often meet with serious moral disapproval from segments of American society—rulings on segregation being a recent case in point.[5] Fundamental tensions between the morally and the legally valid do not occur among traditional Tiruray, for the moral rules are the sole source of any rules recognized as legally valid for purposes of legal action in tiyawan.

Whatever form it may take in various legal systems and whatever institutions it may engender, the existence of a rule of recognition enables the system to authoritatively identify the primary rules of obligation as valid and applicable. In the Tiruray case, the rule that is used by kefeduwan for such identification is the fedew rule, lifted for this purpose from its general usage as a moral basic norm. In other societies, the legal system may employ some quite different form of rule of recognition such as a text or a list acknowledged to be authoritative for this purpose, the declaration of some specified person or body of persons, or past judicial decisions in particular cases. Whatever the form or substance of the secondary rule of recognition, the point is that it strikes, through the legal system, at the problem of generality in the moral system.

Rules of adjudication

KEFEDUWAN have authority to use tiyawan to apply the fedew rule of recognition officially, and they are guided procedurally in doing it by the existence of an analytically different kind of secondary rule, the rules of adjudication.

One who has suffered a bad fedew is directed by Tiruray morality not to blood revenge, although that course of action is recognized as all too possible, but to the way of tiyawan. It is in tiyawan, through the work of the kefeduwan, that the society looks for an official, authoritative decision on the locus and nature of the fault (sala$^{\wp}$) and on the proper satisfaction of desire for retribution (benal). As I have pointed out before, the kefeduwan in tiyawan apply the fedew rule to an evaluation of behavior in such a way that it serves as a secondary rule for the recognition of which pri-

5. The outstanding example, of course, is Brown vs. Board of Education, 347 U.S. 483 (1954).

mary rules apply to that behavior. What is important here is that the kefeduwan do this with society's authorization, and their decisions are accordingly authoritative; persons may opt out of the tiyawan system and prepare to fight the affair out through revenge and feuding, but otherwise they must accept the decisions of the kefeduwan as binding. This capacity to make binding, authoritative decisions regarding fault and restitution derives from and manifests the implied secondary rules of adjudication which grant the authority.

Here we again see clearly that union of primary and secondary rules which Hart suggests is the essence of the legal realm. Whereas the private individual applies the fedew rule privately to his situation as a controlling primary standard and thereby identifies certain primary rules as morally applicable, the tiyawan—following secondary rules of adjudication—applies it officially as a secondary rule of recognition and thereby recognizes the primary rules as legally valid.

Moreover, along with such implied rules of adjudication as those which confer authority upon kefeduwan in tiyawan, custom makes explicit a great variety of these rules in its adjudicatory procedure. Some are institutionalized in the form of standards prescribing procedure: where to hold tiyawan, the value of the seteŋoran in a brideprice, the requiring of brideprice in full in cases of abduction. Others are not formulated, but are implicitly associated with named elements in tiyawan settlement. When kefeduwan, for example, state that an errant husband should give a fedinsel, they do not go on to specify that this means one item of tamuk, usually but not necessarily one necklace, to be given directly to his wife. They do not need to spell this all out, for all of this *is* a fedinsel.

The rules of adjudication, then, are those secondary rules manifested in the granting of adjudicatory authority to kefeduwan in tiyawan and in the structuring of their official procedure. They thereby allow for efficient, *official* satisfaction of the offended party in a dispute.

I have frequently noted that one of the major results of a hot tiyawan is for the kefeduwan to reach agreement on the appropriate extent of the offended party's right to restitution, as expressed in his being awarded certain fine. Any legal system, if it is effectively to take the place of self-help as a reaction to wrongdoing, must adequately provide for the satisfaction of the offended. This is especially crucial in the Tiruray case, as the system does not have compulsory jurisdiction. Revenge killing, while not morally authorized, is always an option.

Honor and standing (tindig) clearly require that some action be taken in response to disrespect, in response to a hurt fedew, for in a real sense one's standing or honor has been called into question. If a person takes no steps to restore his honor, he will in effect accept the implied lower standing. A bad fedew wants to purge the pain and assuage the anger by moving to avenge and justify itself. Tamuk through tiyawan and blood through revenge killing are vehicles—symbols—of vindication. The receiving of an item of tamuk 'to cover one's shame,' the return of one's brideprice, the award of a fine, all represent—like the shedding of blood—more than mere retaliation; they represent public, highly symbolic acts in vindication of standing, of fedew. During the frequent delays and postponements preliminary to the settlement of the case of ?Amig, we witnessed the gradual refocusing of ?Amig's furious concern away from killing and toward tamuk. Both were possible means of "fixing his fedew."

It is thus of great importance that a tiyawan does not seek to arbitrate an acceptable compromise. Its symbolic power to publicly vindicate the offended derives from its strict commitment to justice, to genuine, unbiased determination of right and fault, benal and sala?. Further, the material value of the tamuk which comprises the fine is not the really important thing; what counts is its public symbolic function in recognition and definition of the moral imbalance caused by the fault and in restoration of the moral status quo. Compromise—invariably rejected, as we have seen, as a mode of settlement—could not suffice. The offended would not feel justified by a compromise settlement; his fedew would not be "made good."

Satisfaction of the offended through tiyawan requires and implies satisfaction of general Tiruray moral notions, and there is therefore little tension between popular morality and the popular sense of achieved justice (the latter largely being defined in terms of the former). Indeed, the system could not tolerate such a conflict and remain a viable, satisfying alternative to feuding.

Such a system necessarily puts considerable importance on means of settling inherently hard cases. When fault is absolutely not clear, it has been noted that some uninvolved kefeduwan will announce that he accepts the fault and will give a token fine to the offended person. Tigiʔ (autonomous ordeals) are another such device provided for by the rules of adjudication to deal with situations where the generality problem resists solution, where the rule of recognition cannot be clearly applied. In such ways, Tiruray can handle the challenge of the "ultimately elusive" without recourse to feuding, within the structure of the tiyawan system.

Along with satisfaction of the offended, every society must adequately provide somewhere within its social-control institutions for punishment of the offenders, so that a few malefactors will not take advantage of the obedient majority. There is, however, no formal necessity that the same official agency which adjudicates also impose corrective sanctions, nor, for that matter, that there be any official agency (established by secondary rules) charged with the latter function. The Tiruray case demonstrates this clearly. While the punishment of offenders is indeed accomplished through the Tiruray system, it is not accomplished by the tiyawan, as such.

For Tiruray, matters which bring nonrelatives into conflict are the socially dangerous ones; difficulties between close relatives do not occasion revenge, but are settled by the rebuke of some close elder, by advice, by internalized sanctions of guilt and shame, or by some combination of all of these. Thus tiyawan never occur between protagonists within the same kindred. An individual may behave badly toward a close kinsman, to be sure—he may wrong (dufaŋ) him, cause him a bad fedew, and incite a desire for retaliation (benal)—but the matter is one for family consultation, advice, scolding perhaps, and satisfactory settlement; it is not one for tiyawan. Tiyawan are always between, and never within, kindreds.

It is the specific task of tiyawan to formally relate families in marriage and to deal with interfamily moral breaches. Thus tiyawan come into play in critical situations which the Tiruray understanding

of human nature views as especially dangerous. Through good tiyawan the system structures potentially risky social situations, and
through hot tiyawan it controls actual outbreaks of social disruption.

When an offense causes a dispute between two families, the effect
of tiyawan (in contrast to feuding) is to remove the issue from the
risky between-families context and relocate it within the family of
the offender. Revenge killing both directly punishes the offender
and gives direct satisfaction to the offended; tiyawan symbolically
satisfies the offended, and it symbolically punishes *the offender's
kindred*. There it stops. It is the family of the malefactor (as well
as his own internalized moral code) which rebukes him through
scolding and through the knowledge that he has caused them shame,
the fact that he has cost them tamuk, and the implication that he
has placed them all in danger of blood revenge. It is the offender's
elders and close kinsmen who must accept his fault in tiyawan and
who must bear the burden of his fine. A successful hot tiyawan
ends the interfamily trouble, with all of the social danger it has
threatened, and leaves the wrongdoer in difficulty not with nonrelatives, but with his own closest kin. They may scold him or not;
they may submit him to public advice or not. Either way he knows
that he has been the cause of trouble, shame, danger, and tamuk
loss to his kindred, and this is heavy and embarrassing knowledge.

Thus, one way or another—by vengeance to himself or his family through revenge, by the scolding voice of a kinsman following a
tiyawan, or by the acute discomfort of his internalized sense of right,
wrong, and responsibility—the offending individual ultimately receives his punishment. The administration of corrective sanctions
to the wrongdoer is not, however, the work of the tiyawan. In the
Tiruray system, the function of the tiyawan is to take a socially
dangerous private moral matter (between families) and make of
it first a controlled public legal matter and finally a defused and now
socially safe private moral matter (between the wrongdoer and his
own family).

Application of the rules of adjudication in good tiyawan enables
Tiruray to authoritatively alter the status of individuals from their
initial positions under the primary rules. In hot tiyawan, applica-

tion of the rules of adjudication allows authoritative determination of whether—on a given occasion—a primary rule has been broken. They identify the individuals (kefeduwan), and they structure the setting (tiyawan) by which this authoritative determination occurs. They define the procedure to be followed, and they establish fines in tamuk as the system's official sanctions.

Taken together, the various rules of adjudication form the model *for* official behavior by kefeduwan, guiding their performance as legal authorities in Tiruray society. And, at the same time, they constitute a model *of* what that performance should be, enabling criticism of official behavior by kefeduwan and nonkefeduwan alike.

As with a rule of recognition, secondary rules of adjudication may also be seen as striking at one of the inherent difficulties in the moral system, the maintenance inefficiency of moral rules.

Personal morality, individually applied, cannot establish with authority precisely what happened in the face of transgressions, nor does it arrange efficient counteraction. The absence of secondary rules of adjudication, leaves to the individuals involved such important issues as determination of the offender's identity, of the punishment due him, of the manner in which the punishment should be administered, of the satisfaction due the offended, and of the manner in which that satisfaction should be claimed.

The Tiruray rules of adjudication structure, through tiyawan, a far more efficient legal alternative to self-help for dealing with these issues. These rules grant authority to the kefeduwan in tiyawan for the orderly establishment of marriages and for the orderly settlement of disputes and thus eliminate the necessity, if not the possibility, for wife-stealing and revenge killing.

Clearly, other legal systems employ vastly different structures and rules for their adjudicatory proceedings. As I have noted on several occasions, Tiruray law does not involve adversary proceedings in the conduct of its settlements, thus contrasting substantively with the many legal systems which do. Kefeduwan represent parties only in the sense that they stand ready to identify with them in the acceptance of fault or vindication; they do not contend with each other as juridical opponents.

Furthermore, in marked contrast to many legal systems, the Tir-

uray tiyawan arrangements do not include an official punitive agency. Power, as such, is not characteristic of the kefeduwan role, and,
in the absence of institutionalized power, no effort is made to administer direct punishment of offenders. Nonetheless, the Tiruray
adjudicatory system is legitimate, in that it is operated by officials
accepted by the tribe for that function, according to accepted and
institutionalized secondary rules of adjudication. And the Tiruray
legal system as a whole is authoritative, in that the Tiruray accept
its primary rules as creating genuine obligation and the kefeduwan
accept its secondary rules as binding upon them in the conduct of
tiyawan. It is one of the virtues of the view of law here taken that
power, authority, and legitimacy are distinguished as independent
variables and that no one of them is considered a formal necessity
for the existence of a legal system. The kefeduwan's authority does
not derive from some inherent coercive capacity; he has none. It is
based upon simple willingness of the people to accept his decisions
as authoritative. Fear of an outbreak of self-help violence or, more
recently, fear of involvement with the Maguindanao power structure stands behind that willingness. In other legal systems, popular
acceptance—the only formal requirement of a system's authority
—may stem from any of a great many reasons, of which official
coercive sanctioning power is only one—albeit common—possibility.

The secondary rules of adjudication of one society may set forth
a council of elders with absolute adjudicatory and punitive powers,
they may in another society establish a complex judicial structure
of juries and appellate courts. But, again, whatever the substance
of the adjudication system, its existence permits efficient legal process to authoritatively determine whether and by whom, on a given
occasion, primary rules have been broken; it identifies the officials
to adjudicate, it defines the procedure to be followed, and it provides, in many systems, for centralized and official sanctions.

In short, wherever they exist, secondary rules of adjudication
enable the legal system to ameliorate a second practical difficulty in
the operation of normative common sense: the maintenance inefficiency of moral rules.

Rules of change

FINALLY, law may be seen as remedying a third difficulty, that of the unalterability of moral rules, by institutionalizing the secondary rules of change. In the Tiruray system, such rules are the least developed.

The most straightforward type of secondary rules of change would govern some sort of legislative process by which new primary rules of obligation could be enacted as needed and existing ones could be repealed as they became ineffective or maladapted to the society's needs. Such rules simply do not exist among the Tiruray.

Custom does provide for a kind of change in the obligations imposed by the primary rules: it permits change in one's status under those rules. Through tiyawan, marriages are created and dissolved. Furthermore, there are in Tiruray culture such alterations in status as are involved in the inheritance of certain rights, in the making of agreements, and in the acceptance of promises. The latter are not the subject of tiyawan, but they represent voluntary structures of rights and duties created and observed by persons through mutual consent. Through them, individuals are not frozen into their original relationships vis-à-vis each other under the primary rules, but may redefine, release, or transfer obligations in specific situations. The capacity to do this depends upon common acceptance of private power-conferring rules in the society. Such rules, along with the rules of adjudication which set procedure for a good tiyawan, may therefore be looked upon as constituting a variety of secondary rules of change. They ameliorate one aspect of the difficulty I have described as the unalterability of moral obligations.

Tiruray, however, have no official means of changing custom. There is nothing comparable to a legislative agency with competence to alter the primary rules of obligation. As I have pointed out in discussing the rule of recognition, the source of all legally valid rules is the general moral code. The standards of obligation in the Tiruray system are not codified in a body of law. They remain, analytically, moral rules until one is recognized as legally valid for the purposes of a specific tiyawan. Thus, like all moral norms, they seem to the people for whom they constitute normative common sense to be un-alterable—part of the way the world is. With the slow passage of time, there may be changes in the morality, with certain rules emerging and becoming obligatory and others decaying and falling out of general observance, but moral rules, quite unlike the laws enacted by a legislature, cannot be altered by human fiat.

For this reason the Tiruray system has not been able to overcome the general problem of unalterability. Faced in recent years with a multiplicity of strong forces of change, it has not been able to self-consciously adapt itself to the rapid rise of new conditions.

Tiruray who make the shift in orientation from tribal life to peasant life usually leave their tiyawan system behind. They break away from traditional modes of subsistence and neighborhood interaction and relate themselves anew—nuclear family by nuclear family—first as plow tenants to some landlord, and then through him to all the varied institutions of Filipino peasant life: the schools, the chapels, the clinics, the local government. Other Tiruray, in order to keep the tiyawan system viable, must retreat farther and farther into the mountains and forests—a short-term solution at best. The hope for escape from change is for the Tiruray ultimately vain.

There is no place in the "new world" of peasant life for the kefeduwan. He survives as merely an expert in the stories of the old folks and their customs. Like him, unable to evolve with the speed of today's changing Tiruray world, the elegant tiyawan system of their traditional world seems destined to disappear.

Bibliography and Index

BIBLIOGRAPHY

Bambrough, R.
  1966. Universals and Family Resemblances. *In* G. Pitcher, ed.,
    Wittgenstein: The Philosophical Investigations. A Col-
    lection of Critical Essays. Garden City, N. Y., Double-
    day.

Bennasar, G.
  1892a. Diccionario tiruray-español. Primera parte. Manila, Tipo-
    litografia de Chofre y Compañia.
  1892b. Observaciones gramaticales sobre la lengua tiruray por
    un P. misionero. Manila, M. Perez, hijo.
  1893. Diccionario español-tiruray. Segunda parte. Manila,
    Tipo-litografia de Chofre y Cia.

Berger, P. and T. Luckmann
  1966. The Social Construction of Reality. Garden City, N. Y.,
    Doubleday.

Beyer, H.
  1917. Population of the Philippine Islands in 1916. Manila, n.p.

Bohannan, P.
  1965. The Differing Realms of the Law. *In* L. Nader, ed., The
    Ethnography of Law. Menasha, Wisconsin, American
    Anthropological Association.

Burdett, F.
  1930. The Odyssey of an Orchid Hunter. Edited and annotated
    by Percy J. King. London, Herbert Jenkins.

Commonwealth of the Philippines, Commission of the Census,
  Manila
  1940. Census Atlas of the Philippines. Manila, Bureau of Print-
    ing.

Conklin, H.
    1952.   Outline Gazeteer of Native Philippine Ethnic and Lingu-
           istic Groups. Mimeographed (in the author's possession).
    1955.   Preliminary Linguistic Survey of Mindanao. Philippine
           Studies Program, University of Chicago.

Costa, de la, H.
    1961.   The Jesuits in the Philippines 1581–1768. Cambridge,
           Mass., Harvard University Press.

Geertz, C.
    1958.   Ethos, World-View, and the Analysis of Sacred Symbols.
           Antioch Review, Winter 1957–1958: 421–437.
    1964a.   Ideology as a Culture System. *In* D. Apter, ed., Ideology
           of Discontent. New York, The Free Press.
    1964b.   The Transition to Humanity. *In* S. Tax, ed., Horizons of
           Anthropology. Chicago, Aldine.
    1966.   Religion as a Culture System. *In* M. Banton, ed., An-
           thropological Approaches to the Study of Religion. Lon-
           don, Tavistock Publications.

Gewirth, A.
    1959.   The Quest for Specificity in Jurisprudence. Ethics 69:
           155.

Hart, H.
    1961.   The Concept of Law. Oxford, Clarendon Press.

Hunt, C.
    1954.   Cotabato: Melting Pot of the Philippines. Manila,
           UNESCO National Commission of the Philippines.
    1957.   Ethnic Stratification and Integration in Cotabato. Philip-
           pine Sociological Review 5:13–38.

Irving, E.
    1952.   Physiographic observations on Mindanao by Aerial Re-
           connaisance, and Their Geological Interpretation. Phil-
           ippine Journal of Science 81:141–172.

Jesus, Compañía de
    1877.   Cartas de los Padres de la Compañía de Jesús de la Mis-
           ión de Filipinas. Cuaderno 1. Manila, Imprenta de los
           Amigos del Pais.
    1880.   Cartas de los PP. de la Misión de Filipinas. Cuaderno 3.
           Manila, Establecimiento tipografico de Ramirez y Gir-
           andier.

1883. Cartas de los PP. de la Compañía de Jesús de la Misión de Filipinas. Cuaderno 5. Manila, Imprenta del Colegio de Santa Tomás.

1887. Cartas de los PP. de la Compañía de Jesús de la Misión de Filipinas. Cuaderno 7. Manila, Establecimiento tipo-litografico de M. Perez, hijo.

1889. Cartas de los PP. de la Compañía de Jesús de la Misión de Filipinas. Cuaderno 8. Manila, Tipo-Litografía de Chofré y Comp.

1895. Cartas de los Misioneros de la Compañía de Jesús en Filipinas. Cuaderno 10. Manila, Establecimiento Tipográfico de J. Marty.

Malinowski, B.
1926. Crime and Custom in Savage Society. London, Routledge and Kegan Paul.

Post, U.
The Phonology of Tiruray, Mimeographed (in the author's possession). n.d.

Republic of the Philippines, Department of Commerce and Industry, Bureau of the Census and Statistics
1962. Census of the Philippines, 1960. Manila, n.p.

Saleeby, N.
1905. Studies in Moro History, Law, and Religion. Manila, Bureau of Public Printing.

Savage-Landor, A.
1904. The Gems of the East. New York, Harper & Brothers.

Sawyer, F.
1900. The Inhabitants of the Philippines. New York, Charles Scribner's Sons.

Schlegel, S.
1963. Mission to Mindanao. The Living Church 147:40 ff.

1965. The Upi Espiritistas: A Case Study in Cultural Adjustment. Journal for the Scientific Study of Religion 4:198–212.

1968. Repercussions of Naïve Scholarship: The Background of a Local Furor. Philippine Sociological Review 15:108–113.

in press.   Tiruray Constellations: The Agricultural Astronomy of
            a Philippine Hill People. Philippine Journal of Science.
Schutz, A.
    1960.   Der sinnhafte Aufbau der sozialen Welt. Vienna, Spring-
            er.
    1962.   Collected Papers. vol. 1. The Hague, Martinus Nijhoff.
Stone, J.
    1961.   The Province and Function of Law. Cambridge, Mass.,
            Harvard University Press.
Sturm, D.
    1966.   Three Contexts of Law. Paper read to the meeting of
            the fellows of the Society for Religion in Higher Educa-
            tion, Oberlin.
Tenorio, J.
    1892.   Costumbres de los indios tirurayos, traducidas al Español
            y anotades por un padre misionero de la Compañia de
            Jesus. Manila, Amigos del Pais.
United States Bureau of the Census
    1903.   Census of the Philippine Islands. Washington, D.C., n.p.
Wickberg, E.
    1965.   The Chinese in Philippine Life 1850–1898. New Haven,
            Yale University Press.
Wittgenstein, L.
    1958.   Preliminary Studies for the 'Philosophical Investigation,'
            Generally Known as the Blue and Brown Books. New
            York, Harper and Row.
Wood, G.
    1957.   The Tiruray. Philippine Sociological Review 5:12–39.

INDEX